Happy Birthday
Tommy!

Clark

EPIC ATHLETES
PATRICK MAHOMES

EPIC ATHLETES
PATRICK MAHOMES

Dan Wetzel
Illustrations by Marcelo Baez

Henry Holt and Company
New York

For Kelly Lou Campbell

Henry Holt and Company, *Publishers since 1866*
Henry Holt® is a registered trademark of Macmillan Publishing Group, LLC
120 Broadway, New York, NY 10271 • mackids.com

Our books may be purchased in bulk for promotional, educational, or business use.
Please contact your local bookseller or the Macmillan Corporate
and Premium Sales Department at (800) 221-7945 ext. 5442 or
by email at MacmillanSpecialMarkets@macmillan.com.

Library of Congress Cataloging-in-Publication Data is available.

First edition, 2020

Designed by Elynn Cohen

Printed in the United States of America
by LSC Communications, Harrisonburg, Virginia

ISBN 978-1-250-76231-3 (hardcover)

5 7 9 10 8 6 4

3rd & 16 ▸ KC 13 DEN 23 4th 10:53

1

New Kid in Town

ALL OVER AMERICA, football fans tuned in to get a glimpse of the new quarterback of the Kansas City Chiefs. It was October 1, 2018, week four of the still young NFL season.

They'd heard about the stats—a league-leading thirteen touchdowns in his first three games. They'd seen the highlights—daring passes from an unbelievably strong arm and slalom-like runs through defenders. They'd heard the testimonials about his potential—"the sky's the limit for this kid," Chiefs coach Andy Reid, who doesn't normally praise his players, said after a six-touchdown game in week two.

Now here was a chance to see Patrick Mahomes live on Monday Night Football and judge if he was indeed the potential next big star of the National Football League, or if he was just a flash in the pan whose brief run of greatness would quickly end.

In front of a packed and loud stadium in Denver, Colorado, Patrick put up a solid performance for most of the game. He wasn't great, though. There was no evidence to suggest that he should be crowned king of the NFL or a future Hall of Famer.

He'd thrown for 235 yards and one touchdown. He'd run for another. Respectable, but not special. And as a result, the Chiefs were trailing the Denver Broncos, 23–20 with 4:35 remaining in the game. Kansas City had the ball on their own forty-yard line with the game still in their reach.

Patrick had no time to wait if he was going to lead the Chiefs to victory and make a statement that at just twenty-three years old and in just his first year as the full-time starter, he was a force to be reckoned with.

"Well, these are the moments that can make a guy," the ESPN broadcaster said as Patrick and the offense took the field looking for a game-winning drive. "The moment has arrived for Patrick Mahomes."

It was a moment Patrick had been building toward his entire life.

From as early as he could remember, he didn't just want to be a professional athlete, he expected to be one. He'd grown up around pro athletes, after all. His father, Pat Mahomes Sr., was a longtime pitcher in the major leagues. Patrick would spend summers trailing his dad around, including hanging out on the field before games for batting practice or to shag fly balls.

At first, team officials tried to stop him, assuming a kid that young might get hurt out on the field. Then they saw him chase down a fly or catch a hard ground ball and became so amazed at his skill and courage at such a young age that he earned his place.

Sports quickly became the center of Patrick's universe. There were the baseball games his dad played. Then there were the ones he played—baseball, for sure, but also basketball and football and golf and track and anything else he could compete in. No matter the activity, Patrick almost immediately showed himself to be the most talented among his friends.

"He was a natural," said one of his high school coaches, Adam Cook. "You give him a little while to figure out how a game is played, and he'd beat you at it. Just a natural athlete."

To Patrick, becoming a pro made sense. Why stop playing games once you got older if you didn't need to stop? He didn't even care which sport he played professionally. He just wanted to keep competing and having fun.

As a kid, Patrick assumed he'd be a pitcher. By high school he could fire fastballs in the mid-90s. He could also crack home runs seemingly at will. But it wasn't his only passion.

He loved playing point guard in basketball, leading the team, especially on a fast break. He could also drain long three-pointers and dunk when the opportunity arose. Was hoops his future? Some in his small hometown of Whitehouse, Texas, thought that was his best sport.

Then there was football, where as a quarterback he was able to combine the skills of baseball and basketball—a strong, accurate arm with a knack for finding open teammates with a pass. Soon that became his passion. He loved how each play brought a unique challenge and the need for quick decisions.

It was perfect for Patrick, who played quarterback in his own way—not as a traditional pass-first guy, but also not as a run-first guy. He liked to run, but only to set up the throw. He became known for throwing passes at unusual arm angles and flinging the ball incredible distances.

"He threw the ball like eighty-five yards in practice," wide receiver Tyreek Hill said, noting how he'd never before see anyone toss a ball that far. Almost no one had.

Patrick had become a star at Whitehouse High in East Texas, then at Texas Tech University. Kansas City drafted him tenth overall in the first round of the 2017 NFL Draft, but he spent his rookie year almost completely as a backup, learning from a veteran named Alex Smith.

Then came 2018, and as the team's confidence in him grew, he was named the starter and he immediately showed himself to be a sensation in the making, winning his first three games. At least, that's why football fans far from Kansas City were tuned in to watch him take on the Broncos.

Patrick gathered his team before the drive, and in the center of the huddle, he didn't look like an inexperienced quarterback. He commanded their respect through his talent, of course, but also hard work and humility. He was a team-first player. His guys believed in him.

"Let's go win," he told them.

With over half the field between the Chiefs and victory, Patrick immediately hit wide receiver Tyreek Hill on an eight-yard slant to get things moving. On second down, he threw it to Hill again, but the intense Denver defense tackled Hill for a three-yard loss.

Suddenly it was 3rd and 5 and if Kansas City didn't convert for a first down, they'd have to punt. They might not get the ball back. This single play could determine the game and the sold-out crowd in Denver poured noise down onto the field to distract Patrick and the Chiefs.

Patrick took the snap, but the Broncos' pass rush was ferocious. Denver's best player, Von Miller, a six-three, 250-pound All-Pro linebacker, got free from his block. He began chasing Patrick, who had to sprint to his left to avoid the tackle. Von kept coming, though, and was about to hit Patrick, who had almost no good options.

If Patrick hesitated for another second, Von would sack him and force the punt. If he threw the ball with his right hand, which, as a right-hander, he always did, Von might knock it out and cause a fumble. So Patrick did what perhaps only he could think of doing, let alone actually pull off. While on the run he switched the ball to his *left* hand and then sort of pushed the ball through the air to Tyreek, who was a few yards downfield.

Patrick released the ball just as Von tackled him. The ball fluttered through the air and into the hands of Tyreek, who quickly turned up field for the first down. All over the stadium, all over the country, people couldn't believe what they had just seen.

A left-handed throw by a right-handed quarterback?

"How did he pull that off?" said one ESPN announcer.

"Are you kidding me?" said another announcer on the broadcast. "Wow. This guy is incredible."

"I thought, 'Is he a magician or something?'" Chiefs running back Kareem Hunt said.

"Whoa," said Chiefs coach Andy Reid. "That was pretty good."

It was more than pretty good. It was *incredible*.

"I was kind of just scrambling left," Patrick explained. "I felt Von on my back and I knew I couldn't throw it with my right hand and I knew we needed a first down. I just shot-putted it to Tyreek. You just have to get the ball in their hands somehow."

It was a highlight reel play few were capable of matching, but all it did was earn a first down. The Chiefs were still nowhere near the end zone and the clock was ticking. And it wasn't like Von Miller and the Broncos defense were going to quit.

After a couple of penalties, Kansas City was in even worse shape—facing 2nd and 30 with 2:59 remaining. The Denver pass rush again came after Patrick who had to scramble right to buy some time before chucking it on the run to receiver Demarcus Robinson for twenty-three yards. It was another amazing pass.

Now on 3rd and 7, Patrick needed some more magic. Thankfully he had some left in the tank. Rather than get just past the first down chains, he again scrambled right, away from more Denver tacklers, and heaved the ball down field for a thirty-five-yard completion.

The Broncos couldn't believe what was happening. Neither could football fans. Three consecutive unbelievable throws by Patrick Mahomes! A few plays later, Kareem Hunt scored on a run and Kansas City took a 27–23 lead that they wouldn't give up.

The Chiefs won. All anyone could do was talk about Patrick and his improbable passes.

"Some amazing plays there," said Coach Reid. "We've seen it in practice, but not under those conditions. He's a confident kid, he's a confident player."

Patrick just shrugged and praised his teammates. He didn't want the focus to fall on him.

"[The victory] speaks about how much heart we have," Patrick said.

He didn't need to brag. The message had been sent. He proved that not only was the hype real, but this new kid in Kansas City was just getting started.

2
Early Years

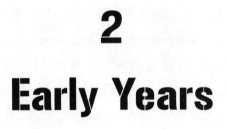

PATRICK LAVON MAHOMES II was born on September 17, 1995, to Pat and Randi Mahomes. Randi was an event planner, which meant she organized and threw parties for people. Pat Sr. played baseball for the Minnesota Twins. He was a relief pitcher, specializing in entering games when the Twins were leading and then shutting down opponents.

Being a pro athlete was exciting, but it didn't leave much time for family. The day after his son was born, Pat Sr. was back at work, pitching three and one-third scoreless innings.

That was the family's way, though—it was always about being dedicated to their jobs. Pat Sr. hadn't even played competitive baseball until his senior year of high school in Texas. He thought he would attend college to play basketball, not baseball. Once he showed some promise, however, he worked his way up to become a major leaguer.

Nothing was given to him and no one thought he'd make it. He wound up playing eleven seasons for the Twins, Boston Red Sox, New York Mets, Texas Rangers, Chicago Cubs, and Pittsburgh Pirates. It was that kind of determination, work ethic, and self-confidence that Pat Sr. would instill in his son.

Patrick was the firstborn, followed by brother Jackson. While their dad was playing baseball around the country, their mother raised Patrick and Jackson in Whitehouse, Texas.

Whitehouse is a small city of about eight thousand in East Texas, about halfway between Dallas and Shreveport, Louisiana. It is a suburb of nearby Tyler, Texas, and is surrounded by woods and lakes. It's the type of place where everyone seems to know everyone and life revolves around local high school sports, especially on Friday nights in the fall when the football team plays. Wildcat Stadium seats seven thousand, so almost the entire city could come to a game and have a seat.

"I was blessed to grow up in a great community," Patrick said.

Both Patrick's mother and father had been raised in Tyler, so they were surrounded by family. His mother felt comfortable while Pat Sr. was off playing baseball. In the summers, Randi and the kids would join Pat Sr. in whatever city he was playing.

In addition to his father, Patrick's godfather, LaTroy Hawkins, was also a professional baseball player. LaTroy and Pat Sr. were best friends. LaTroy would play twenty-one years in the majors. As a result, Patrick was surrounded by pro athletes at a young age, including teammates and even opponents of Pat Sr. and LaTroy.

Patrick and Jackson loved being around the game of baseball. Both got to serve as bat boys for their dad's teams and spent plenty of time during games hanging out in the dugout or running around the stadium. Sometimes they'd shag fly balls during batting practice or play catch with other major leaguers. It was a dream childhood for a sports-loving kid.

"I was actually one of the first guys with the Mets

to bring a kid on the field [before games]," Patrick's father told the *Fort Worth Star-Telegram*. "Everyone was scared he'd get hurt."

It didn't take long for Patrick to prove he could protect himself. He was such a good young athlete, even at twelve or thirteen, that he could catch flies and knock down ground balls from major leaguers, shocking everyone with his ability. Soon everyone stopped worrying about this young guy getting hurt and instead watched as he chased down a fly ball like a high schooler.

"Patrick was allowed to be on the field because he could catch a major league pop-up," LaTroy told *Bleacher Report*. "The ball wasn't going to hit him in the face when he was knee-high to a grasshopper. He could handle his own."

Patrick thought it was cool to meet the best players in the game. But it was more than just a cool experience; though he may not have realized it at the time, he was also learning crucial lessons about how hard someone needed to train and focus to be a professional athlete. He saw the things they did and then tried to act the same way in his games. While the job is a lot of fun, it also requires incredible dedication.

"I watched Alex Rodriguez. I watched Derek Jeter," Patrick said of two all-time great players. "I watched firsthand and [saw] how much work they put in every single day. It really showed me that you can be at the top of your game and you still have to work every single day if you want to be great."

Patrick recalls spending a lot of time with Alex Rodriguez, who was his dad's teammate in Texas. A-Rod was a fourteen-time All-Star in his career and considered one of the best to ever play. Yet despite his fame and accomplishments, he still took the time before games to teach Patrick how to be a better player.

"He would watch my swing and give me some pointers," Patrick said. "It was awesome to have a guy like that take an interest in me."

Pat Mahomes Sr.'s MLB career ended in 2003, when he was cut by Pittsburgh. He didn't stop playing, however. He loved the game too much, so he agreed to report to the minor leagues, where the competition is a bit easier. The pay was much smaller, but Pat Sr. just couldn't stop competing. He played six more years before calling it quits in 2009, when he was thirty-eight years old and Patrick was fourteen.

Growing up, Patrick and Jackson would spend

many of their summers living in cities where their dad was playing minor league baseball, such as Las Vegas, Nevada, Nashville, Tennessee, and Sioux Falls, South Dakota. When fall came, they'd return to Whitehouse so they could attend school. For one stretch, Pat Sr. even played in Japan. The family followed him there and got to experience a new culture, although the kids didn't love the local food.

"I was too young to remember much about Japan except I ate at McDonald's a lot," Patrick said.

If anything, the minor leagues were even more fun for Patrick and his brother because the game is a little less serious than the majors. One time in Sioux Falls, Pat Sr. was on the mound pitching when he noticed neither Patrick nor Jackson was in the dugout. He grew concerned and began glancing around the ballpark searching for them. He finally spied them on a fan party deck singing karaoke!

But as much fun as he had, Patrick also faced struggles during his childhood. When he was six years old, his parents decided to get divorced. They remained close and even as they got into new relationships, it still felt to Patrick like one family. Years later Patrick would have two new sisters, Mia from his mother's side and Zoe from his dad's. While Patrick and Jackson were growing up, they had both parents involved in their lives. However, much of the time, Randi had to raise the kids alone and deal with the challenges of being a single working mother. Patrick took notice of her sacrifice.

"The biggest influence my mom gave me was just hard work," Patrick said. "Every single day doing her job, going to my games and just being there. Just being a mom. It just shows me that whatever your situation, if you work hard you can be successful."

It wasn't easy. Patrick was a bundle of energy every day, always strong for his age. He'd eventually grow to six-three. Jackson was four and a half years younger than Patrick, but would eventually stand six-five, and like many younger siblings, never wanted to let his older brother get the best of him.

The result was a house where all types of games—basketball, football, baseball, wrestling, you name it—were being played at nearly all times, with no location off-limits, including their backyard, game room, and driveway. The Mahomes brothers were constantly crashing around the house, and games would get so heated that they routinely ended in fights. It seemed like every day the two of them were breaking something.

The front door. Lamps. Even the oven in the kitchen.

"What kid breaks an oven?" Patrick's mother told the *East Texas Sports Network*. "I mean, shatters an oven. I never would buy new stuff before Patrick moved out because I was like, 'they're going to break it.'"

Patrick's mother needed to find him an outlet for all that energy, so she signed Patrick up for nearly every sport, league, or camp she could find. If there was a ball involved, Patrick was doing it. He didn't mind. He loved to play anything, although he was most interested in basketball, football, and, of course, his dad's sport, baseball.

Patrick was always at the center of every team. He was a quarterback in football, a point guard in basketball, and a pitcher and shortstop in baseball. One year, when he joined a Pop Warner football team, the coach made him play linebacker instead of quarterback. Frustrated by his change of position, Patrick told his parents he wanted to quit. But that wasn't the Mahomes way, and his parents saw an opportunity for an early, important lesson: They told him he had to listen to the coach and do what was best for the team.

He was a gifted athlete, faster and stronger than the other kids his age. His father would often tell people a story of Patrick playing T-ball when he was five or six years old. According to the story, Patrick fielded a ground ball at shortstop and threw it so hard to first base that the first baseman couldn't catch it. The ball then hit the first baseman in the head, knocking him down. Patrick moved up in age groups soon after that.

He was so talented that his mother was almost immediately convinced he would make it big one day.

"I knew he'd be a professional athlete when he was 7," Randi told the *Kansas City Star*. "I'm serious. There was never a question. I knew he had the talent."

Patrick hoped she was right. When adults asked him what he wanted to be when he grew up, he always gave the same answer, "pro athlete." He didn't care which sport, as long as he was a pro. And he wasn't interested because of the money or fame either. He just loved playing sports and figured why stop? When someone mentioned trying something else, he just shook them off. He was an excellent student, so he had a backup plan, but he was determined to follow his dream.

"I always wanted to be a pro athlete growing up," Patrick said. "I never took no for an answer. I compete in everything I do, school, schoolwork, on the field, on the court."

That competitive drive was only just beginning to blossom.

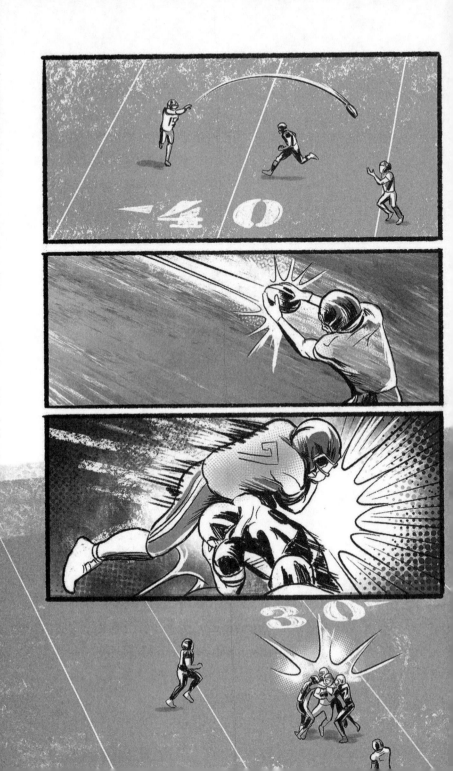

3

Multi-sport Athlete

EVERYONE ASSUMED PATRICK would eventually focus exclusively on baseball, like his father and god-father. At the time, Patrick thought that as well. Yet he also didn't want to give up playing other sports quite yet.

By middle school, if not sooner, lots of young athletes specialize in one sport, often due to pressure from coaches. Travel teams want players who participate all year round. The alternative, they often tell kids and their parents, is that they'll fall behind if they don't stick with a single sport. These teams also operate as businesses, so the more a kid plays and practices, the more they pay.

Patrick and his family saw it differently. First off, Patrick just wanted to have fun. No matter the sport, his priority was learning, playing, and trying to keep getting better. He always wanted to win at everything. He also felt that lessons he learned in one sport often aided him in other sports, too.

"I've always believed in playing as many sports as you can and just compete," Patrick said. "Just go out there and just be a competitor. I think that is what got me here in football. You see things in baseball, you see things in basketball. I played everything growing up. Just that competitiveness and finding a way to win. It doesn't have to be perfect fundamentals."

To Patrick, playing a game of Ping-Pong in a friend's garage could feel as important as an organized travel baseball game all the way across Texas.

"I just always wanted to compete and win games," Patrick said. "I just always wanted to be the best growing up."

One time he and his friend Ryan Cheatham played a game of washers against one of his middle school and high school football coaches, Brad Cook, and Brad's wife. Washers is a simple backyard game people play during cookouts or at football tailgates. It consists of trying to throw small metal circles (washers) into a cup that rests inside a box. It's usually just a fun way to pass some time.

"Not with Patrick," said Brad Cook. "He wanted to beat us and he kept playing until he could. Even on something like that, he had only one goal . . . to win. There was no such thing as an easy game with him."

Patrick couldn't imagine an athletic competition going down in Whitehouse that he didn't want to be part of. He wasn't alone either. Patrick had a pack of friends who played alongside him, shifting from one sport to the next as the months of the calendar passed. There were a lot of good athletes in Whitehouse then, but four stood out as friends and teammates: Ryan Cheatham, Jalon Dews, Jake Parker, and Coleman Patterson.

They were nearly inseparable, on or off the playing field or court. They began to create the chemistry and trust that would carry across sports. A certain cut to get open on the basketball court would be duplicated in a football game.

At one point, they formed the starting five for a

junior high–age basketball team that played around East Texas. Years later, Patrick was the starting quarterback of the high school football team and his four wide receivers would be the same guys—Ryan, Jalon, Jake, and Coleman.

"I think it built a brotherhood, that was the biggest thing," Patrick said. "We played basketball, baseball and football together. You could see that bond. It was why we ascended to heights we never even thought we could ascend to.

"We all played baseball," Patrick continued. "We all played basketball. They were my wideouts. It kind of started there with my creativity. They would run routes and then change the route because they knew how to get open. And I was on the same page with those guys. Those guys are still around. I still hang around those guys when I go home."

For Patrick, it helped that he excelled at virtually everything. It wasn't just baseball, basketball, and football. He became an ace in Ping-Pong. He could make a Wiffle Ball bend in crazy directions. He could crush a golf ball. He could soar in the high jump in junior high school. Even in his main sports, he'd do things that seemed impossible. Patrick batted right-handed in baseball, but sometimes he'd go up there and hit lefty just for fun. More than once he hit a home run that way as well.

"He was that kid in gym class that could just do everything better than the other kids," said Coach Adam Cook, Patrick's high school football head coach.

Coach Cook believed that Patrick improved in all sports by playing more than one sport. Whatever is lost in not having the perfect form or technique is made up for in learning different skills and strategies that can be applied to different games. That was his advantage, especially in football. He played the game like no one else played it because he learned to play the game like no one else learned it.

The sidearm throws as a quarterback? That was Patrick on the pitcher's mound or racing to get a throw across from deep in the hole at shortstop. "There were times he threw it 50 yards with what looked like a flick of the wrist," Adam Cook said.

The no-look passes or the hip shakes past defenders into open space? That was Patrick in the open court as the basketball point guard, trying to find space and teammates who could score easily.

"He'd come down on the break, look a defender off and pass it for an easy basket," Cook said.

But beyond the translatable skills, the most important lesson was just the will to win. Whatever it took, Patrick found a way. Instead of spending all his time practicing and practicing and working on fundamentals, he was competing and playing and figuring things out on his own. If he had specialized in being a football quarterback, he'd have only played maybe ten games in an entire year. Jumping from sport to sport allowed him to learn the different ways to win.

"Patrick is the poster child for the multisport athlete," Adam Cook said. "Because he played multiple sports, the overlay of all of those experiences and skills are there. The mindset for young athletes shouldn't be, 'I can do it. I can play multiple sports and not just specialize in one.' It should be, 'I need to be doing it. I need to be playing all these games and getting all the experience I can.'"

Adam Cook noted that being a multisport athlete won't make a regular athlete into Patrick Mahomes. It's just that being a multisport athlete made Patrick Mahomes into Patrick Mahomes. It maximized his talents.

"I think playing lots of sports helps with the competitiveness you have to have," Patrick said. "That helped mold me to be the kind of quarterback that I am. Obviously shortstop, having to throw sidearm accurately and basketball having to play in space and still make the passes really helps me in my game."

Back in middle school, a lot of people in Whitehouse believed Patrick's best sport was basketball, where he was a great shooter and terrific floor leader. Others thought it was baseball. No one thought it was football, including Patrick.

"Football was my number three sport," he said.

High school was still to come, though.

4

High School

BY THE TIME PATRICK reached middle school he was known as the best athlete for his age in town. Word of this young phenom had even reached the football coaches at Whitehouse High School.

"I heard some youth coaches talking about how there was a kid in town who was in the sixth grade who was a really good athlete," said Adam Cook, who was the Whitehouse offensive coordinator at the time. "They said his dad was a professional baseball player, Pat Mahomes.

"Everyone was excited to have an athlete like

that, but no one knew what sport he was going to play in high school," Adam Cook said.

That summer, before Patrick was set to enter seventh grade, he attended the Whitehouse football camp. Coach Cook remembers two things about it. First was at the start of camp, when Patrick walked in wearing a baseball cap backward. It wasn't a big deal, but the football team had a rule that all caps needed to be worn facing forward.

"I said, 'you're going to have to turn that hat around,'" Coach Cook said. "Patrick just did it. He didn't say a word, he just did exactly what he was told and I never saw him wear a cap backward again. He understood the rule and followed it without complaining. That was impressive."

Then came the drills. Patrick was just twelve years old but his ability popped off the field. The way he ran. The way he threw. The way he competed.

"We started doing drills and you could see the kid had serious talent," Coach Cook said. "You could see he was very good and was going to be very, very good."

Later on, as a freshman, Patrick didn't play varsity football. Size matters in football and Whitehouse had enough older, larger players to fill out a varsity roster. He did make the varsity team in basketball and baseball, however.

In basketball, Patrick was the point guard, the floor general, always setting up plays. He wasn't particularly fast, but he was great at changing speed and keeping defenders off balance. He was also shifty, had great vision of the court, and was a very good shooter.

"He was so smart," Whitehouse basketball coach Brent Kelley told *Bleacher Report*. "If he wasn't shooting it well, he'd get you in the post and just control his body. Make you do something—draw a foul, get to the free-throw line. Late in games, we'd get the ball in his hands . . . he was versatile. Great passer. Unselfish."

In both Patrick's junior and senior seasons, he averaged over nineteen points a game. When he was a senior, Whitehouse went 28–7, and in consecutive playoff games Patrick scored an impressive thirty-seven and forty-nine points.

Still, Patrick's chances of making it in pro basketball weren't great. While his eventual height of six-three is generally considered tall, in the NBA, he'd be considered small. While he was a terrific player, hoops wasn't going to be his professional future.

Baseball sure seemed like it might be, though. Patrick was an instant starter on the Whitehouse team and over the course of his four years started a game at every position except catcher. He was best as a shortstop and a pitcher, two of the most important positions, but his coaches appreciated how he'd do anything to help the team.

As a pitcher Patrick was known for his fastball and his ability to use different angles to confuse batters. "The fastest I got up to was 96 miles per hour," Patrick said. "I could throw it pretty hard. I'm not going to say I had great control, but I could throw it."

He had good enough control of the ball to be the team's best pitcher. And as a shortstop, he was great at chasing down grounders and whipping the ball to first for an out. As a batter, he hit an amazing .450 his senior year. He did it all.

Maybe the best display of his abilities came on a day when Whitehouse High was scheduled to play two games, back-to-back, against two different opponents. In the opener, he was the starting pitcher. He struck out sixteen batters and threw a no-hitter as Whitehouse defeated Mt. Pleasant, 2–1. Then hours later, he went 3 for 4 at the plate, including recording a home run and three runs batted in, as Whitehouse defeated Princeton, 10–3.

"He [could] do pretty much anything he wanted on the baseball field," his baseball coach at Whitehouse, Derrick Jenkins, told *MaxPreps*.

In fact, his baseball talents were in such high demand that the Detroit Tigers selected him in the 2014 Major League Baseball draft even though Patrick hadn't committed to playing the sport full-time and wanted to play college football. The Tigers figured he was worth the gamble because if he did wind up choosing baseball over football, they'd have a steal of a pick.

During high school, however, football began to become increasingly important to Patrick. As a sophomore, he made varsity, although he wasn't named the starting quarterback. Whitehouse had a senior who was returning, a kid talented enough to go on and play college football at Stephen F. Austin State University in Texas.

Patrick could have spent the year as a backup quarterback who only occasionally played in games. Instead he told the coaches that he wanted to get out on the field and help the team in any way possible. Patrick had played some wide receiver growing up, catching passes from his friend Ryan Cheatham, who was also a good quarterback.

However, Whitehouse really needed help on defense.

The coaches thought Patrick was a strong enough athlete to play safety in the defensive backfield. Patrick agreed and became the starter.

"I don't think he liked playing defense a whole lot, but he loved to compete," Coach Adam Cook said. "He never pouted about not being the quarterback. He was never like that."

Not only did it reiterate to Patrick's coaches and teammates that he cared about team success more than individual success, playing defense actually turned out to be an advantage for him. Patrick learned to view the game from a different perspective than just quarterback.

"He had a knack for knowing where the ball was," Coach Adam Cook said. "He wasn't naturally a defensive-minded player but the experience showed him how defensive-minded players thought. That was a big help when he returned to playing offense."

Entering his junior year, Patrick was battling his friend Ryan Cheatham for the starting quarterback job. Growing up they each played quarterback and wide receiver—sometimes it was Patrick passing to Ryan and sometimes Ryan passing to Patrick. Both were good players and as the season started, no one knew who would wind up being the starter or if they'd end up alternating. Patrick threw for three touchdowns in each of Whitehouse's first two games, both victories. Ryan was also good in those games, however. Then came the third game, against Sulphur Springs. That's one that people still talk about, the one that cemented Patrick as not just the starter, but a potential star.

Patrick threw for 403 yards and one touchdown and rushed for 105 yards and three touchdowns to lead Whitehouse to a come-from-behind 38–33 victory. He began to show the ability to throw the ball on the run, scramble past defenders, and invent plays at a moment's notice. One of his touchdown runs spanned nearly half the field, forty-eight yards. It became clear he needed to be the full-time starter. Ryan moved mostly to wide receiver, where he became a dangerous weapon for Whitehouse.

"It was like a light flicked on with him," Coach Adam Cook said. "It was under the Friday night lights, big home crowd, and he just played incredible. That was when you knew he was born to play football. He played like the Patrick Mahomes that everyone now knows."

The next game, Patrick threw five touchdown passes in a victory over Marshall. Then five more in a victory over Lindale. Then five more in a victory over Nacogdoches. In a win over Corsicana, he threw six. Suddenly Patrick and Whitehouse were unbeaten and getting all sorts of attention, climbing the state rankings and drawing not just big crowds to Wildcat Stadium, but college recruiters who wanted to witness the Patrick Mahomes Show in person.

There were just two disappointments that season. A loss to nearby rival John Tyler High School (despite Patrick throwing four TD passes and rushing for another). Then a second-round playoff defeat to Wylie East (despite Patrick throwing five TDs).

Still, Patrick finished the season having thrown for 3,839 yards and forty-six touchdowns. He also rushed for 258 yards and six TDs.

Unlike many future college stars, whose recruitment processes begin as soon as they enter high school, it wasn't until his junior season that Patrick got the attention of college football coaches. Remember, he hadn't even played quarterback until then. Plus he spent his off-seasons playing basketball and baseball, not going to football camps or playing 7-on-7 ball, as is common among many future college players. His ability in baseball, and the fact that his father had been a big leaguer, also scared off some of the major schools in Texas. They thought he'd turn pro for baseball after graduating high school.

His junior season was so impressive, however, that some college coaches began to call and visit in an effort to get Patrick to play for them. One of them was Kliff Kingsbury, who was the new coach at Texas Tech University. Coach Kingsbury was in his midthirties, young for a college head coach. He'd been a star QB at Tech and later a backup to Tom Brady with the New England Patriots. He favored a wide-open offense and a creative quarterback who could pass and run.

It didn't take long for him to see Patrick and know he wanted him to come to Lubbock, Texas, and play for the Texas Tech Red Raiders. And it didn't take Patrick long to realize that Coach Kingsbury would be the perfect coach for him. Besides, Tech had a powerhouse baseball program and everyone agreed Patrick could play both sports. In April of his junior year, Patrick committed. As quickly as it'd begun, his recruitment was over.

"Really excited about Patrick," Coach Kingsbury said when Patrick officially signed with Texas Tech. "Dynamic athlete, three sport star. And he's a winner. You watch him play and he willed his teams over and over . . . when you see him in person, he's a big, impressive kid, and I think he's going to get bigger, stronger and faster."

Indeed he would, but there was still his senior year of high school left to play.

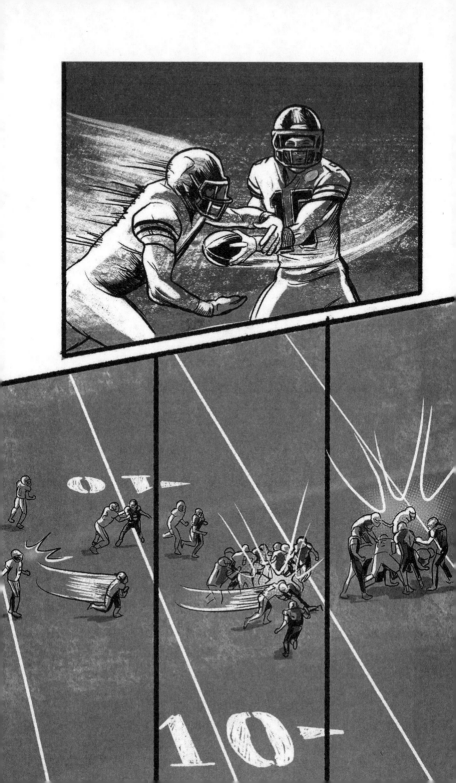

5
Senior Year

THE WHITEHOUSE HIGH SCHOOL football team had a motto: "Keep Swinging."

The message was simple. It didn't matter if a player was running sprints during off-season conditioning, or struggling with technique in the heat of a summer practice, or trailing late in the fourth quarter of an actual game. They needed to just keep going, keep pushing, keep *swinging*.

The coaches even bought a sledgehammer to serve as a symbol of the team's mindset. Each week, a player would be chosen to charge out of the locker room and onto the field carrying that sledgehammer. It was considered an honor.

As Patrick's time with the team ticked on, Coach Adam Cook noticed something. Patrick had never carried the sledgehammer or led the team out on the field. Every time he had been chosen or it had been discussed, he'd found a way to convince the coaches to pick someone else.

One week he suggested a kid who needed a boost of confidence. The next it was someone who had worked extremely hard in practice that week. Patrick even suggested team managers. He clearly knew this was a big deal and he wasn't trying to be disrespectful in refusing the honor. He thought it would be an even bigger deal to someone who likely wasn't headed to college or the NFL.

"He just knew, 'that's for the other guys, I get enough attention,'" Coach Adam Cook said. "It wasn't until late in his senior year when he finally did it. And that's because we made him. He didn't care. Patrick just always wanted it to be about the team. When we'd take the field pregame, he always went last. He wanted the other guys to get the cheers. He was a natural leader."

Patrick wasn't just the best football player at

Whitehouse High School in the fall of 2013. He was the best football player ever at Whitehouse High School. But he barely ever acted like it—except when the game was going on.

Then he was dashing around, throwing touchdowns, avoiding sacks, and winning games. Yet he was never one to call attention to himself. He didn't celebrate a touchdown with some look-at-me dance. Instead he'd go congratulate a teammate. And when local reporters wanted to talk to him after the game, he'd spend more time praising his offensive line, defense, or wide receivers.

"There would be a play where he'd make an incredible throw or he'd scramble around and make a big run for a touchdown and he'd come off the field saying to his teammates, 'great catch' or 'great block,'" said Coach Brad Cook, the team's offensive coordinator. "He'd say it even if most of the reason the play was successful was because of his throw or his ability to elude tackles.

"It didn't matter to Patrick, though," Brad Cook continued. "He wanted to lift up his teammates. It was all about the team and he figured that if he could improve their confidence then the team would play better. I also think he knew he was good. He was very confident in that, but he didn't need to talk about his performance. He knew his play would speak for itself. As a coach, and for a team, that is just an incredible thing to have from your best player."

It was a sign of not just who Patrick was, or how he was raised, but his determination to have the best season possible. This was what he and his friends had been building toward their whole lives. He knew that no matter what came afterward—college football and baseball, the pro ranks in some sport—there was nothing quite like senior year of high school.

The team started strong and Patrick was better than ever. Four touchdown passes and one running the ball in a 58–28 victory over Hallsville. Four touchdown passes and one running the ball in a 42–34 victory over Chapel Hill High out of Tyler. Then four touchdown passes in a 61–22 clubbing of Sulphur Springs. That's just how it went, game after game, and no one could figure out how to shut down Patrick.

"He was just always making the right decisions out on the field," Coach Adam Cook said. "When he needed to stay in the pocket and pass, he would. When it was time to scramble and run, he would. He was unstoppable."

Whitehouse defeated Marshall 59–3 behind five touchdown passes from Patrick. The next week, they beat Lindale 63–7 behind five more TD throws and two TD runs. Then came a 70–21 beating of Jacksonville, where Patrick had two rushing and two passing touchdowns.

"He could have had even better stats if the games were close," Coach Brad Cook said. "We'd take him out of the game when it got out of hand."

Patrick credited his coaches for helping him grow comfortable on the field. He wasn't a traditional quarterback who just dropped back three steps and threw the ball. He needed to come up with plays on his own, try daring throws, or tuck it and run when needed. He was at his best when he felt free.

"Coach Adam Cook was a great figure in my life when I was young," Patrick said. "Being in high school and being a baseball player who was playing football, he was the first guy to show me how to play the quarterback position. He didn't force me to be a certain type of quarterback, he let me go out and just play the game how I like to play it."

The reason was simple: Coach Cook knew that Patrick, being a multisport athlete, hadn't learned to play quarterback in the usual manner. So why try to box him in like a traditional quarterback? Especially when the results spoke for themselves?

They beat Nacogdoches to go to 8–0. Then they defeated Corsicana to move to 9–0. Then came a showdown against rival John Tyler High School, which is located in nearby Tyler, Texas. The game would go down in history around Whitehouse.

It was tied 48–48 late in the fourth quarter. Whitehouse had the ball, but their passing attack was being stifled. Every time Patrick dropped back, his receivers were covered. So over and over, he just tucked the ball under his arm and ran.

"I told Coach Cook, 'Coach, just keep calling it. I'm going to get in there,'" Patrick told the East Texas Sports Network after the game.

He finally did on a fourteen-yard run that capped a twelve-play, sixty-eight-yard drive. Whitehouse led 55–48, but John Tyler wasn't done. They drove down and scored a touchdown with 59.8 seconds left to make it 55–54. John Tyler then decided to go for two and win the game in regulation, but the Whitehouse defense made the stop. Whitehouse won, 55–54.

"That's one of the greatest games you'll ever see," Coach Adam Cook said.

In the wild shootout, Patrick threw for 391 yards and five touchdowns, and rushed for eighty-five yards and two touchdowns.

Whitehouse finished the regular season 10–0, and Patrick and his friends entered the playoffs seeking a Class 4A, Division 2 championship. It wouldn't be easy, of course. High school football in Texas is huge, and Whitehouse would need to win six games against some of the best teams in the state to do it.

First up was a game against Seguin High School, which is located in Arlington, Texas, right between Dallas and Fort Worth. Whitehouse was favored to win, but these were the playoffs. Seguin came out and played a great game, and thanks to a twenty-one-point fourth quarter, held a late 44–37 lead.

It looked like Whitehouse's dream season might come to an end in the very first round of the play-offs. For Patrick and the others, this was a potential nightmare. In the final minute of play, Whitehouse was facing 4th and 8 on the Seguin twenty-eight-yard line. If Whitehouse got stopped, the season would be over. This was the kind of pressure that can cause even great athletes to fall apart. Patrick saw it differently.

"I don't think there is any added pressure," Patrick

said. "It's just about going out there with your team-mates, your brothers, and playing the game that you love. If you are doing this the right way and enjoying it, then you are just going out there with your team-mates and knowing that it is a blessing to be out there. The biggest thing with adversity is keeping a positive attitude and then leaning back on your training and fighting through it."

On that 4th and 8, Patrick dropped back to pass, but he couldn't find anyone open. He looked left. He looked right. Everyone was covered. As the pass rush closed in, he stepped into a gap and raced away from three Seguin defenders. At that point, he decided to tuck the ball under his arm and make a play himself. He charged past the first down line but wasn't satisfied. He kept running toward the goal line, breaking one tackle at the eight-yard line, another at the three-yard line and then carrying two additional defenders into the end zone. Whitehouse kicked the extra point—tie game!

In overtime, Whitehouse got the ball and quickly scored again for the win. Patrick finished with five touchdowns (two throwing, three rushing).

"Patrick just wouldn't allow us to lose that game," Coach Adam Cook said.

After dispatching Sulphur Springs in the next round of the playoffs, Whitehouse matched up with Poteet High School in round three. Poteet is a town in South Texas, but the game was played on a neutral site in a suburb of Dallas. The game was a thriller, each team roaring down the field and scoring almost at will.

Patrick was incredible, throwing for 619 yards and five touchdowns and rushing for two more scores. Poteet's quarterback, Lane Novy, was equally great, throwing six touchdowns himself. In the end, Poteet just barely edged out Whitehouse and won 65–60. There wasn't anything more Patrick could have done.

The loss was a huge disappointment, the end of a great run for Patrick and his friends. "Playing football with those guys all those years were some of the best times of my life," Patrick said.

That's how it is, though—there can only be one champion.

But for Patrick, something even bigger was on the horizon.

College football.

6

Texas Tech

WHEN PATRICK ARRIVED at Texas Tech, the football program was going through major changes. The 2013 Red Raiders had gone 8–5 in Coach Kingsbury's first year. It was a good record, but it had been an uneven season. Tech won its first seven games. Then it lost five in a row.

The star of the team was freshman quarterback Baker Mayfield, who had arrived at Tech as a so-called walk-on, which meant he hadn't been given a scholarship and little was expected of him. Instead he won the starting job and went on to be named Big 12 Freshman of the Year.

Mayfield's development was exciting for Tech fans, but it wasn't necessarily good for Patrick. Mayfield was just one year older, and if he was going to be the long-term starter, that meant Patrick might struggle to get on the field. Unlike some positions, there can only be one quarterback at a time. Because of Baker's development, two backup quarterbacks decided to transfer out of Tech in search of other opportunities.

Then Baker surprised fans by deciding he, too, wanted to transfer out—to the University of Oklahoma. It was a big blow to the Tech program. Mayfield was a dynamic player who at Oklahoma would lead the Sooners to the college football playoffs, win the Heisman Trophy, which is presented to college football's best player, and wind up the number one pick of the Cleveland Browns in the 2018 NFL Draft.

For Patrick, though, this was a golden opportunity. There was now only one returning quarterback with any experience on the roster, Davis Webb, who would be a sophomore in the fall of 2014 when Patrick was a freshman. Davis was a good player, but the depth chart was now very thin.

Football is a physical game, where injuries are

common. Patrick hadn't expected to play much as a freshman, but now, before he even stepped foot on campus, he was the second string. All of a sudden, instead of sitting back and getting adjusted to college football, Patrick was going to play.

"I hope so," Coach Kingsbury said. "We're going to play him as much as we can. When we can find times that he can go in the game throughout the year, we're going to try to maximize that."

Texas Tech has a sprawling campus just west of downtown Lubbock, Texas, a city of about three hundred thousand that sits in the state's flat, dusty panhandle. The area is known for growing cotton, ranching, and oil production. Lubbock isn't a big city, but it's the biggest for miles and miles—the closest major city is Fort Worth, and that's about a four-and-a-half-hour drive to the east.

Texas Tech sports, and football in particular, are very popular in the area. It's not just students or alums that follow the Red Raiders. It feels like the entire city and surrounding area are fans. There aren't a lot of other entertainment options. Fans come from all over to fill the school's sixty-thousand-seat Jones AT&T Stadium. It is a very exciting place to be an athlete.

Patrick showed up ready to work. During football summer camp, he immediately impressed his coaches and teammates, not just with his natural athletic ability, but his work ethic and willingness to learn. Often star high school players get to college and think they have everything figured out. Patrick arrived humble. He knew there was only one way to make it work . . . by putting in the effort to improve.

"He's a coachable kid," said Davis Webb. "Coach Kingsbury gives us footwork every day, and the next day he's fixed it. It's there, it's done. He listens to everybody. He's kind of like a sponge . . . Pat's really smart, and he understands guys who are older than him know more than an eighteen-year-old freshman does . . . he wants to learn to be the best."

Patrick didn't play in any of Tech's first three games that fall. Davis Webb started and took every snap. As the Red Raiders began 2–1, Patrick adjusted to the speed and demands of college football. The intensity of the game was much higher in college. Even in practice, every snap or repetition was done with incredible intensity.

In the fourth quarter of the team's fourth game against Oklahoma State, Davis Webb scrambled from a pass rush only to jam his shoulder awkwardly on the turf. The medical team came out to examine him and soon slowly walked him off the field.

Coach Kingsbury called for Patrick to enter the game and begin his career. Tech was trailing by ten points, playing on the road in a game that was broadcast on national television. It was facing a third down with twenty-four yards to go. As debuts go, this was not ideal.

"He's going to get a baptism of fire, here," said one announcer on ESPN, who mispronounced Patrick's last name.

"A true freshman that just learned the system?" agreed another announcer, expressing more doubt.

Patrick faced a 3rd and 24 from deep in his own territory, so his first play was a designed run where he scampered fourteen yards. It would've been a forgettable play if not for the fact that Patrick showed some of the running ability that he would later become famous for.

The next time Tech got the ball, Patrick was determined to do better. What became immediately clear is that he wasn't ready to run a college offense. The speed of the defensive players was unlike anything he'd seen in high school. That meant he needed to make lightning-quick decisions on where and when to throw the ball.

On the first two plays he couldn't find an open receiver and scrambled from the pass rush. On the third, he fumbled the ball, scooped it up, and then, rather than make the safe play, tried to make a daring one. As he was falling down, he chucked the ball blindly to what he thought was an open receiver. Instead the ball was tapped in the air and picked off by an Oklahoma State defender.

Patrick Mahomes's first college pass was intercepted.

That wasn't a very good way to introduce himself to Texas Tech fans, but he wasn't alone in throwing a pick on his first-ever pass. Future Baltimore Ravens star Lamar Jackson also threw an interception on his first college pass while at the University of Louisville. Same for the New England Patriots legend Tom Brady when he was at Michigan. Even worse, Tom's was returned for a touchdown.

For a lot of freshmen quarterbacks, such a mistake would rattle them, cause them to lose confidence and impact their play the rest of the game. Patrick just shrugged it off.

"You can never allow the last play to impact the next play," Patrick said.

This is where his baseball background paid off. In baseball, a batting average of .333 is considered excellent. If you can do that, you are a star player. To hit .333 means one hit in every three at bats. That also means two out of three times, the batter messes up.

All those strikeouts and groundouts over the years teach baseball players to put failures behind them and focus on the next at bat. In baseball, you are supposed to stumble. Patrick had learned that not just playing the game, but sitting in dugouts with his father and watching even superstar players such as Alex Rodriguez ground out and then brush it off.

Patrick saw that first interception as nothing more than a first-inning strikeout. There were more chances at the plate coming, and as long as he didn't lose his confidence, he could still hit some home runs.

On the next possession, he did just that, tossing a touchdown pass. He finished the game with two completions for twenty yards and another sixteen yards rushing. While no one watching would think that a future NFL star was making his debut, it was a start.

Davis was healthy enough to play in Tech's next game, but he threw four interceptions as the Raiders lost 45–13 to Kansas State. With the offense stalled and Texas Tech with little chance of coming back,

Coach Kingsbury decided to give Patrick another chance to play. He went 5 for 7 for fifty-four yards, but more importantly, he was beginning to look comfortable out there.

A few weeks later he was back in the game, this time when Davis injured his leg in a lopsided 82–27 loss to Texas Christian. The game was terrible for the Red Raiders; their defense couldn't stop TCU. The eighty-two points didn't just break the record for the most points ever scored by a Big 12 team, it caused fans all over the country to pay attention to the game. Such an uneven score is almost never seen.

By the time Patrick got in, the game was hopeless. He went just 5 of 11, with one touchdown and one interception. His play was better than his stats, though.

"Yeah, not bad," Coach Kingsbury said. "I thought he stepped up and made a nice play on the touchdown."

The biggest development, however, was that unlike the shoulder injury, Davis's leg injury was serious. That meant Patrick, ready or not, was suddenly the starting quarterback heading into a rivalry game against the University of Texas. Coach Kingsbury expressed some confidence in his freshman.

"I think Pat does a good job," Coach Kingsbury said. "He's an accurate passer and does a good job extending plays with his feet [by scrambling away from defenders]. I think that's something he really excelled at in high school and has continued to do . . . in our system."

Patrick dreamed that his first start would result in a Red Raider upset of Texas. Here was a chance to make a statement as a freshman starter.

Patrick played well enough, going 13 of 21 for 109 yards, until he got hit on a rollout by Longhorn defender Quandre Diggs. That jarred Patrick's head and he went down, unable to continue. Tech had to go to their third-string quarterback and lost, 34–13. The team fell to a disappointing 3–6.

Up next, mighty Oklahoma, traditionally one of the best teams not just in the Big 12, but all of America. OU won, 42–30, but Patrick began to show everyone exactly what he was capable of doing. He threw for 393 yards and four touchdowns. He also rushed for thirty-one yards. He spent much of the day scrambling around and extending plays. Most importantly to Coach Kingsbury, he didn't turn the ball over once, either by fumble or interception.

"He created with his feet, kept some things alive

under some tough rushes," Coach Kingsbury said. "Just proud of the way he battled. Wasn't always pretty, missing things. As a young guy, the way he kept fighting, the moment wasn't too big for him."

There was more, too. Patrick looked like a starting quarterback. He carried himself with confidence, and that, in turn, made his teammates confident in him. He may not have been polished or experienced enough to dominate a game, but it was clear that time could come.

"He's a very confident young man," Coach Kingsbury said. "He's been great at everything he's ever done, whether it be baseball or basketball. He's just very confident in his abilities."

Patrick said that it was actually Coach Kingsbury's belief in him that helped Patrick believe in himself.

"For him to have that confidence in me gave me confidence that I could play at that level," Patrick said.

That confidence only increased the following week, when Patrick threw for 328 yards and four touchdowns in a big, 34–31 victory at Iowa State. The last one was a forty-four-yard strike to running back Kenny Williams that gave the Red Raiders their final lead. For a team that had lost seven of its previous eight games, the victory was a big relief.

"He's got a lot of competitive spirit," Coach Kingsbury said. "He always thinks he's going to win and he thinks he's the best player every time he goes out there."

Texas Tech's season finale was against number five–ranked Baylor, which was still contending for both the Big 12 and national championships. It was the toughest opponent of the season for a team that was just 4–7. Little was expected of the Red Raiders.

Patrick didn't care. He went out and had a remarkable game, throwing for 598 yards and a whopping six touchdowns. No freshman had ever done that in Big 12 history.

Still, it wasn't enough. Baylor held on to win, 48–46, when a Tech two-point conversion fell short. Tech finished 4–8, a disappointing season overall, but there was plenty of optimism in Lubbock when it came to the quarterback position. In his final three games as a starter, Patrick had thrown for 1,319 yards and fourteen touchdowns.

Baker Mayfield may have left, but Patrick Mahomes had arrived.

7
Breakthrough Season

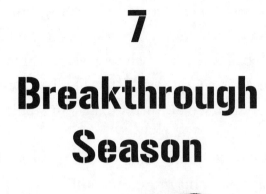

PATRICK'S FRESHMAN SEASON had given him a new perspective on his future. He had always been such a great athlete that he could play three or more different sports in a year and excel in all of them. He even felt that taking time away from one helped him return even more motivated.

Playing college quarterback was different, though. It required reading confusing college defenses and recognizing almost immediately where to throw the ball, sometimes before the ball was even snapped. That meant lots of studying film, meeting with coaches, and endless repetitions in practice.

It was part of what he loved about football. Every play was a chance to create something. Every play was an opportunity to try something different.

"Baseball, I felt like I almost peaked," Mahomes told the *Kansas City Star*. "I felt like I knew everything about baseball. In football, I'm still learning something every single day."

In the winter and spring of 2015, Patrick began to focus more and more on football. His performances at the end of his freshman year, especially against Baylor, had given him a morale boost.

"There was some momentum," Patrick said. "It kind of gave me a little bit of confidence that I could compete against the best in the country. That momentum I guess it gave me a little bit [of motivation]."

He had come to Texas Tech to play baseball, too, but he found himself struggling to juggle the responsibilities of both sports. He was often late for baseball practice because he had been at the football facility. He was also extremely focused on his academics. While most people saw him as just an athlete, Patrick also wanted to be a real student.

And he was—just a very, very busy one.

"I've been very impressed with the way he's

handled going to baseball one day and then going to football the next," Coach Kingsbury said. "And that's hard on an 18-year-old kid. Especially one with a 4.0 [grade point average, which equals all As]."

But as the demands of Patrick's schedule piled up, baseball started to take a backseat to everything. Tech had a very strong team and spent most of the season nationally ranked. It was hard for any freshman to crack the lineup, especially one who spent the fall playing football rather than being completely focused on baseball. Patrick wound up making just one appearance as a pitcher and only got up to bat twice.

It was clear that football had begun taking over.

Texas Tech fans spent most of the off-season discussing and debating who would be the starting quarterback in 2015. Patrick had been very good at the end of the year, but he only became the starter because Davis Webb was injured. Davis was now healthy, and if he had beaten Patrick out once, would he do it again?

During training camp, Coach Kingsbury wanted the two of them to have a fair competition, and officially never said who the starter was going to be, even when badgered by fans or reporters. He did, however, quietly let the players know. By the middle of summer camp, his mind was made up.

Patrick would start. Davis would be the backup, but needed to be ready to step in at a moment's notice if Patrick didn't prove himself worthy.

"He never really just said it, said it," Patrick said. "I don't think he ever really just said 'you're the guy, you're the starter' . . . It really didn't change anything. Davis is a great quarterback, so either way I was just going to compete every single day."

Patrick started the season hot, throwing for a combined eight touchdowns (plus two rushing) in victories over Sam Houston State and the University of Texas at El Paso (UTEP). That led into Tech's biggest challenge outside of conference play, a road game at Arkansas.

The year prior, Arkansas had blown Tech out, 49–28, in Lubbock, setting the tone for a losing season. "You don't forget a beating like that," Coach Kingsbury said. Tech wanted to prove they were better now, even if the game would be played in Arkansas's rowdy seventy-six-thousand-seat stadium.

Few who watched the game would forget the performance the Red Raiders put on. The defense stuffed Arkansas's powerful running attack that had steamrolled them the year before. Meanwhile Patrick was nearly flawless, going 26 of 30 for 243 yards and one touchdown pass. He also rushed for fifty-eight more yards, delivering on countless critical third downs and scoring two more touchdowns.

Final score: Texas Tech 35, Arkansas 24.

The Red Raiders were 3–0. The losing season in 2014 was behind them, and Patrick and the team were starting to get some national attention. Back in Lubbock, fans immediately sold out their next home game against Texas Christian, which was ranked number three in the country.

The game proved as exciting as anyone could want. TCU opened with an eighty-yard touchdown drive. Texas Tech responded with an eighty-six-yard touchdown drive. TCU scored another touchdown. Texas Tech answered again. On and on it went. There were eleven lead changes, a combined 1,357 total yards of offense and even a safety (by TCU).

When Patrick hit Justin Stockton for a 50-yard pass to give Tech a late 52–48 lead, the biggest victory in years for the Red Raiders seemed possible. TCU made a late drive, however, reaching the four-yard line with just twenty-three seconds remaining.

That's when QB Trevone Boykin threw it into the end zone, had his pass tipped by one TCU receiver, and then fell into another just before he fell out of bounds.

Touchdown. TCU 55, Texas Tech 52, in one of the wildest games anyone had ever seen. While plenty of people were entertained, especially the national television audience, Patrick and his teammates were dejected. They had wanted to prove they were for real, and beating the third-ranked team in America would have done it. Now they were 3–1, and just a footnote on TCU's winning season.

This was the story for most of the season. Tech had improved greatly during Patrick's sophomore season, but while they could now defeat some of the weaker teams in the Big 12, they still struggled, especially defensively, against the good ones.

They beat Kansas, Kansas State, and Iowa State, but lost to Baylor, Oklahoma, and Oklahoma State. The regular season finale was against rival Texas, on Thanksgiving night. Could they finally beat the Longhorns?

The one thing that wasn't in doubt was Patrick's play and his leadership. He was making plays no one had believed possible, all while hobbled with various injuries. No matter how many times he got knocked down, he always got back up.

"Pat is a soldier, just the energy he plays with, the spirit," said teammate DeAndre Washington. "Not only does he get the offense going, he gets the whole team going. Just to see him going out there, sacrificing his body the way he does and making those special plays, man, it's an energy you can't really explain."

Patrick remained positive no matter what happened each week. The offense was generally very good, but the defense's struggles were often too much to overcome. The Red Raiders gave up sixty-three points in losses to Baylor and Oklahoma and a whopping seventy to Oklahoma State. There is almost no way to win a game when you allow that many points.

Yet Patrick never blamed them or began talking bad about anyone. Not during the week, postgame, or even during the game. If the defense allowed a quick score, he would just put his helmet on and get the offense ready to go out there and answer with a score of their own. Patrick knew that he wasn't perfect—he threw interceptions and sometimes missed open receivers. So why focus on someone else's mistake?

As a result, a team that could have splintered stayed together.

"He doesn't change," said Tech center and team captain Jared Kaster. "He's the same demeanor that he is throughout the whole game. That's what you want. That's what you want in a quarterback that is in a position that he's in. It fires us up.

"You could say it's rare," Kaster continued. "But from knowing Pat, it's just him . . . being around Pat as long as I have, it's just Pat. I mean, Pat is Pat."

Meanwhile, the coaches had begun to appreciate Patrick's full range of talent. Those scrambles weren't just lucky plays, so they started designing the offense around his ability to run and avoid tackles.

Then there were the times he did things you wouldn't normally allow a quarterback to do, such as throwing the ball across his body. When a QB runs right and then on the fly throws left, the ball usually lacks speed and can be easily intercepted. Pat's arm was so strong, however, that he routinely laced passes to Tech receivers.

"He's better at [throwing across his body] than anybody I've ever seen, which is remarkable," said the team's offensive coordinator, Eric Morris. "[H]e's pretty special. It's fun to watch him create these plays and find people downfield, and how accurately he throws the ball on the run is what's really remarkable to me."

Now that Tech was matched up against the Longhorns, it was time to make this season truly matter. When it comes to college football in the state of Texas, the University of Texas is the most famous, the most popular, and has the most tradition. It has won national titles and lots of conference championships. Its home stadium seats over one hundred thousand. The Longhorns had won six consecutive games against the Red Raiders. Patrick wanted to make this season different.

Early in the second quarter, with Texas leading 3–0, Patrick threw a deep ball all the way across the field—the kind of risky pass only he could sometimes make. At first it looked like a mistake that would lead to a turnover. A Texas defender jumped in the air and seemed ready to intercept the ball. As he came down with the ball, though, he was hit. The ball flew out of his hands and up into the air, where Tech receiver Jakeem Grant swooped in, grabbed it, and raced sixty-five yards for a touchdown.

With that, the shootout was on. Texas would come back to tie it. Then Tech took the lead again.

Then Texas went ahead. Then Tech answered. It went back and forth like a tennis match. There were six touchdowns scored in the fourth quarter alone. Patrick threw for one touchdown and ran for another as he moved the Red Raiders up and down the field. Running back DeAndre Washington picked up 173 yards and two touchdowns.

Late in the fourth, Tech led 41–38 but knew it needed one more touchdown to put the game out of reach. Even with just over two minutes remaining, it didn't want to give the ball back to the Longhorns with the chance to tie or win.

Jakeem Grant stood just five foot seven and weighed just 168 pounds, tiny by college football standards. He was as fast as lightning, though. If you could get him the ball in open space, he could make defenders miss and gain yards.

On 1st and 10 from the Longhorn forty, Tech ran a trick play, featuring Jakeem. They packed their big offensive linemen close together and had Jakeem crouch behind them, so none of the defenders could see him. He was just too small. Patrick quickly took the snap from center and immediately handed the ball to Jakeem. Then Patrick ran directly backward to confuse the defense and two of his receivers ran to the right side of the field.

Texas didn't realize what was happening, and when they finally noticed Jakeem scampering around the corner with the ball it was too late. He raced into the end zone to give Tech a 48–38 lead.

"I just knew that if I put it in Jakeem's hands . . . we would score," Patrick said.

Tech would go on to win 48–45, breaking a number of losing streaks to Texas and showing everyone that this Red Raider program was having a lot of fun.

"At Texas Tech we don't beat Texas at Texas a lot so that was awesome," Patrick said.

The Red Raiders were 7–5 on the season, good enough to reach the Texas Bowl in Houston and play Louisiana State University (LSU). The trip was fun for the team, although the main focus was on using the three weeks of practice before the game to get a head start on the 2016 season. LSU, usually one of the best teams in the country, would win the game, 56–27. Patrick was able to throw for four touchdowns, but the speed of LSU was too much. He was sacked six times.

The loss did little to tarnish the season. The 586 points scored was the most by any team in school history. The offense ranked second nationally in scoring offense (45.1 points per game), total offense

(579.5 yards per game), and passing offense (388.2 yards per game). It also led the country in plays that gained at least ten yards—284 of them.

Patrick himself led the nation in total offense, finishing with 5,112 yards gained, 4,653 of them by air. At the time, he was just the thirteenth player ever to break the five-thousand-yard mark. He also accounted for forty-six total touchdowns (thirty-six passing, ten rushing). And he was back and armed with plenty of experience.

If Texas Tech could improve its defense, a problem that new coaches and additional recruits were expected to solve, then it could be a dangerous team in 2016.

Everything was in place. Or so it seemed.

8
Football Focus

PATRICK HAD ALWAYS enjoyed playing football, especially quarterback. The roar of the crowd. The thrill of breaking a tackle. The joy of hitting an open receiver downfield. In many ways it was the ultimate team game, and Patrick loved competing alongside his teammates.

Across his sophomore season at Texas Tech, his appreciation of the game began to deepen. It was no longer just the games that he loved, or even the high-energy practices. It was the small stuff—studying game film, breaking down defenses, meeting with

Coach Kingsbury about what needed to be accomplished in the next game.

Playing quarterback is an unpredictable challenge; you never know exactly what will happen on a play, and that spoke to Patrick. It challenged him mentally by making him prepare for every scenario. And it challenged him physically because at any given moment he might need to improvise. To him, football was everything, and because of that he wanted to try to learn everything about it.

He was about to turn twenty-one years old, and it was becoming obvious that to lead Tech or pursue a professional career, he needed to dedicate himself full-time to one sport, either baseball or football.

What once felt like an impossible decision no longer was. He didn't just want to play football, he wanted to study, learn, and live football.

"It was a very hard choice," Patrick said. "I was just having too much fun playing football and I knew I could never give it up. So I chose football even though a lot of people told me to choose baseball."

His father, the baseball player, wasn't surprised.

"He just fell in love with football," Patrick's father told the *Star-Telegram*. "I knew that. Thousands of people in the stands, being the man who could dictate and change the game. He's a student of whatever he's playing. He had played baseball for so long, he knew every situation . . . There was so much for him to learn in football and that's what he loved."

Patrick's plan to focus on football paid off almost immediately. Across the winter and spring of 2016, there were noticeable improvements. The most obvious was with his throwing motion. Playing baseball, especially pitching, as a kid and in high school had built up his arm strength. That helped him become a great quarterback. However, throwing a football and throwing a baseball require different arm motions. Switching back and forth between the sports required Patrick to relearn the way to throw whatever ball he was throwing. Now he could spend his time fine-tuning exactly how he tossed a football.

"It has helped me mechanically," Patrick said. "Playing baseball and football, my mechanics would get wild. My release would be wrong. Just focusing on football and being in the film room and getting that extra work in."

It's not that he didn't miss baseball. He did. He even had to watch from afar as the Tech baseball team reached the College World Series that spring for just the second time in school history. Even then he didn't regret his decision.

"I know how much it takes to be a good quarterback," Patrick said. "Back in high school, I wasn't big on watching film or anything like that. You get here and you realize that everybody is good, it's just a few good players on a team, everybody can play. You have to study. It's like another class, really."

Whereas his mechanics needed work, there had never been any doubts about Patrick's arm strength. That summer, Patrick had shocked the Internet when video emerged of him throwing a ball sixty-five yards in the air . . . while kneeling. People couldn't believe that it was real.

Patrick took no vacations during the spring and summer of 2016. He mostly stayed in Lubbock and went to the football facility daily. About his only trip off campus was to attend the prestigious Manning Passing Academy in Louisiana. The Academy is run by the Manning Family, which includes former NFL quarterbacks Archie (the father) and Peyton and Eli (the sons).

Archie was a star with the New Orleans Saints from 1971–82. Peyton was named the Most Valuable Player in the NFL a record five times and won Super

Bowls with the Indianapolis Colts and the Denver Broncos. Eli won two Super Bowls himself with the New York Giants. The three of them combined threw over one thousand touchdowns in the NFL.

The weeklong camp allows not just the Mannings to teach young quarterbacks how to play the position, but includes other NFL stars and many of the top pro and college coaches in the country who work as counselors. Patrick had never attended before, since prior to that point he was always busy playing baseball while the camp was in session. Now with this golden opportunity, he tried to soak everything up like a sponge.

Perhaps the most impactful tidbit he learned came from Peyton Manning himself. Peyton told him that he had to become nearly addicted to watching film, and while watching it, he needed a notebook in hand to jot down observations. Manning said the key was not just scouting opposing defenses, but to watch film on your own play and figure out what you did wrong.

"At the Manning Passing Academy you go out there and have fun but once the competition kicks in, [you] want to be the best guy out there," Patrick said. "You kind of joke around and talk about it and talk trash but when you get to a competition setting, you go all out."

By concentrating exclusively on football, Patrick had also worked to get physically stronger. All those early morning sessions in the weight room with his offensive line transformed his body. He went from 220 pounds to 230, adding nothing but muscle.

"I turned myself into a meathead, trying to get big, trying to lift more weight than the guy next to me," Patrick said with a laugh.

Patrick also spent considerable time in a small room inside the football offices. The room was dark, with a couple of computers and green turf running wall-to-wall, like a carpet.

It was there that Patrick would strap on a virtual reality headset, grab a football, and run through various plays.

What he saw was essentially what he would see in an actual game, defenders charging at him, receivers running routes, and decisions needing to be made in an instant. The room was just big enough for him to mimic taking a snap and perfect his footwork inside the pocket as a pass rush collapsed around him. Patrick loved the experience and found it more valuable than just watching plays shot from sideline cameras on a computer screen.

"The virtual reality, I'm right there seeing exactly what I see when I'm taking my drops and making my throws," Patrick said. "Just being able to see their defenses from my perspective before I even play them, it really does help out. I can basically take my drops and go through my reads and my progressions."

It was innovative and cutting edge, especially in 2016, but Coach Kingsbury was a true believer.

"It puts you at the quarterback position and it's like a flight simulator for a pilot. You're getting those reps mentally that there's no other way to simulate that," Coach Kingsbury said. "[Y]ou see the play and then you signal it out. With the thing on you can see the leverage of the DB's, see the front, see the blitz, see the safeties."

Coach Kingsbury was such a strong believer in Patrick's ability to grow with this tool, that he thought Patrick might prove to be the best quarterback in America in 2016.

"I think you will see a much more refined, athletic, polished quarterback this fall," Coach Kingsbury predicted. "If what I saw this spring translates to the field this fall, then he will have a very special year."

It wasn't just Coach Kingsbury who thought that. As the season approached, the excitement about the Tech season extended far beyond Lubbock. Patrick found himself on a number of national player and quarterback of the year watch lists, essentially predicting a big season.

Meanwhile, Coach Kingsbury and Patrick even appeared on the cover of *Dave Campbell's Texas Football,* a magazine in Texas that is widely read by football fans. To appear on the cover is considered prestigious.

Patrick just shook off the fan attention and ignored the media predictions.

"Our goal is to win the Big 12," Patrick said. "That's it. Not go to a bowl. It's to win the Big 12."

9

Junior Year

On a hot, humid, West Texas Saturday night, Patrick and his teammates donned special, all-black uniforms—black helmet, black jersey, black pants. They lined up in the tunnel that leads into Jones AT&T Stadium before charging through clouds of smoke onto the field. In front of them was the Masked Rider, a Tech mascot who wears all black, except for a red cape, and who rode out onto the field atop an all-black horse.

They were greeted by the roars of over sixty thousand fans. The opponent that night was Stephen F. Austin, a team from a lower division of college football that wasn't expected to offer much competition. That didn't matter to Tech fans, who couldn't contain their excitement for the start of what they hoped would be a big season.

That September night was everything you could want in a college football environment, and Patrick and his teammates didn't disappoint once the game began. They thumped Stephen F. Austin, 69–17. Patrick scored six touchdowns, four throwing and two running. Tech gained 758 yards of total offense, the fourth-highest total in school history.

The numbers felt like something out of a Madden video game. This offense was almost unstoppable, and if the defense, which had been Tech's problem under Coach Kingsbury, could stop opponents the way it stopped Stephen F. Austin, then a successful season was possible.

But despite the landslide score, Patrick was hardly satisfied. "I could have definitely done a lot better," he said.

He'd need to be better in the next game, a major nonconference matchup at Arizona State. This would be the big early-season test for Tech to determine if it would be able to compete with the top teams in the Big 12.

Tech had a promising start against Arizona State. ASU scored a touchdown on its opening drive, but after that the Red Raider defense stiffened for the rest of the first quarter. Meanwhile, Patrick scored on a one-yard run and then hit Derrick Willies for a fifty-nine-yard touchdown.

Then the dam burst. Arizona State began gashing the Tech defense, moving the ball and scoring at will. State put together six consecutive touchdown drives, each of them fifty yards or longer.

This had been the fear going into the season, that the defense would break down and make it almost impossible for Tech to win. ASU's Kalen Ballage scored an NCAA-record eight touchdowns all by himself.

Patrick and the offense did its best to respond, but by the fourth quarter, the Arizona State lead was too big. Tech tried to mount a comeback, but they essentially needed to score a touchdown on every possession, which proved impossible.

Patrick threw for an incredible 540 yards and five touchdowns, plus that one rushing TD, wowing fans and NFL scouts. Yet it wasn't nearly enough. Arizona State won easily, 68–55. Just like in 2015, Tech was let down by its defense. It's almost impossible to win a game when you give up sixty-eight points.

"We're disappointed in how we played defensively," Coach Kingsbury said. "But I believe in those guys."

Patrick focused on how the Tech offense didn't score on every possession and how a nonconference loss had no impact on their goal of winning the Big 12 Conference (where only games against other league teams counted).

"I told the team after the game, we did lose the game and it's disappointing, but we went out," he said. "We still have the things that we want [to accomplish] in front of us. We can still . . . win games if we want to."

Patrick threw for five touchdowns and ran for another in an easy win over Louisiana Tech. He threw four more to help beat lowly Kansas and run Tech's record to 4–1. During the game, however, he injured his shoulder after getting tackled at the end of a thirty-two-yard run. As he lay on the turf with trainers and doctors around him, a hush fell across Tech's home stadium. Everyone knew that if Patrick was seriously injured, the season was in jeopardy. There was also concern about Patrick's professional future.

The injury was diagnosed as a shoulder sprain.

He was out for the rest of the Kansas game and was expected to miss four to six weeks, right as Tech was set to play their most crucial Big 12 games. Patrick, however, took rehab seriously and progressed quickly. Thanks to Tech's schedule having an off week, he was able to use the extra time to return far earlier than expected, in time for the next game, against Kansas State.

"A lot of guys would not have played in that game," Coach Kingsbury said. "He wanted to play."

Patrick's shoulder was still sore, and he appeared to tire late in the game. He still managed to throw for 504 yards and two touchdowns while running in three more. But the Herculean effort wasn't enough. Kansas State scored on a ninety-nine-yard kickoff return and a pick-six to win 44–38.

With that, the Texas Tech season began to fall apart. The Red Raiders would lose four of the next five games, with opponents scoring at least forty-five points each time. No matter how many touchdowns Patrick produced in the air and on the ground, it was never enough. He was one of the best and most exciting players in the country, but Tech wasn't built, especially on defense, to win games.

"I've never seen a team play that poorly, coaches

coach that poorly, and just get embarrassed," Coach Kingsbury said after a lopsided loss to West Virginia. "So I have to apologize to the fans, student body, alumni. That was as bad as it gets."

A season that began with great hope and a team that believed it could contend, if not win, a Big 12 championship behind its star quarterback, crumbled into a series of humiliating losses.

About the only bright spot is the team kept trying to get better. Patrick was battered throughout the season, yet even with the shoulder injury he never missed a game. It's a true testament to Patrick's remarkable mindset that he never backed down an inch despite the crushing disappointment of the season.

The most memorable game of the year came in late October, when league powerhouse Oklahoma came to Lubbock. The Sooners starting quarterback was former Red Raiders quarterback Baker Mayfield. Baker wanted to come back and show Tech nation what they were missing. Meanwhile, his old Tech teammates wanted to prove they were better off with Patrick.

The atmosphere was intense. The Texas Tech student section greeted Baker with some negative chants, which he said just motivated him. "I enjoyed it," Baker said. "It makes it fun." Lubbock isn't too far from the Oklahoma border, so there were plenty of Sooner fans there to see their favorite team.

For Patrick, the rivalry wasn't as intense. He wanted to win, but he and Baker were friends. When he came to Tech on his recruiting visit, Baker was his host. Baker still had friends on the Tech team and would come back to Lubbock in the off-season to hang out. Patrick always joined them. His goal was to win for his teammates, not beat Baker.

What transpired was the greatest show of offense in the history of college football. Patrick and Baker would go on to become starting quarterbacks in the NFL, and this night showed why.

Baker completed 27 of 36 passes for 545 yards and seven touchdowns! The touchdowns piled up so high that he said he lost count during the game. Meanwhile OU running back Joe Mixon rushed for 263 yards and two touchdowns while also catching four passes for 114 yards and three more touchdowns.

Tech wasn't going to be silenced either. Patrick threw for 734 yards (tying an NCAA record) and five touchdowns. He also ran for eighty-five yards and two more scores, giving him an NCAA-record 819 total yards of offense. His passing stats were unheard-of, including attempting eighty-eight passes, which would tire out just about any other arm on the planet, let alone one that was recovering from injury.

Each team gained 854 yards. The combined 1,708 total yards set another NCAA record for one game. It was like no defender on either team could tackle. Each offense just slung it around like it was a pickup game down at the park.

In the end, even with all the yards and scores, Tech still couldn't win. Other than when it ran out the clock on its final possession, Oklahoma scored every time it got the ball in the second half and triumphed, 66–59.

It was a bitter loss for Tech, but is fondly remembered by college football fans for the electric offensive performances, the crazy stats, and the incredibly high-level quarterback play from Baker and Patrick.

"I wish we would have won, but it was just awesome to be a part of it," Patrick told *Sports Illustrated* years later.

Heading into its final game of the season, Tech was just 4–7. There would be no Big 12 championship. There would be no bowl trip. This was just a losing season. Patrick, however, wouldn't stop trying to rally his teammates. The season had been disappointing. He was banged up—he added a knee injury along the way. But getting down on teammates or giving up wasn't going to help.

"You try to be positive," Patrick said. "You can get on people, but at the same time, you've got to be positive. Just tell them that you leave it all out there, take it one game at a time, do your job, leave it on the field, and that's all anyone can ask for."

Sometimes leadership gets praised on winning teams. It's a lot easier, though, to lead teams that win. Almost everyone is happy and motivated when victories pile up. One of Patrick's great attributes, and why his teammates always believed in him, was that he continued to be positive and forward-thinking, even when most Saturdays brought a loss. He was clearly the best and most talented player on the team, yet he never acted that way.

With multiple injuries and a season going nowhere, he could have easily sat out the finale against Baylor. Resting up and avoiding injury would have been smart. Patrick would have a choice to make after the season—return for his senior year or leave Tech and make himself eligible for the NFL draft.

If he was planning to go the NFL route, then playing the game was a big risk. He didn't want to risk suffering an injury that might scare NFL teams away from selecting him.

Not only did he never consider skipping the Baylor game, he spent the week in practice pushing everyone like Tech was playing for a championship.

"For me, it's trying to win games for my brothers," Patrick said. "Trying to send these seniors out the right way and go out there and play as hard as I can and leave it out there."

He certainly delivered against Baylor. Patrick threw for six touchdowns, including passes of sixty-two, eighty, and eighty-one yards. It was another wild game, with the two teams combining for 1,300 yards of offense, but this time Tech did enough to win in an upset, 54–35. After tons of disappointment, their bad season ended on a high note.

Patrick finished his junior season with 5,052 yards passing and 285 yards rushing, making him the second player in NCAA history to post two seasons with over five thousand yards of total offense. His 421 yards per game passing led the country. He also had forty-one touchdowns passing and twelve rushing despite numerous injuries.

He won the Sammy Baugh Award, which is presented to college football's top passer and was a finalist for a number of other honors. The one his parents were most proud of, though, was when he was named Academic All American and the Big 12 Scholar-Athlete of the Year. That meant that while working relentlessly to be the best quarterback he could be, he also worked just as hard on his studies.

With the season over, Patrick had a decision to make. Stay in Lubbock for one more year or head to the NFL. While some people saw a talented player on a mediocre team and figured it would be an easy decision to turn pro, they didn't understand how much Patrick cared about his school, his coaches, and his teammates.

"Leaving the program early would be hard," Patrick said. "I love it here. I love Texas Tech."

The decision would be complicated.

10
NFL

EVER SINCE HE was a young kid tagging along with his father to Major League Baseball stadiums, Patrick dreamed of being a professional athlete. Finally, he was on the cusp of making that longtime dream a reality.

The National Football League has a system where they ask teams about specific college players and then inform the players where they might get drafted. Or if they aren't going to get drafted at all. That way an underclassman such as Patrick, who could return to school, would be able to make an informed decision. When the NFL said he'd be picked in the second round, at worst, Patrick knew what he had to do.

He officially declared himself eligible for the 2017 NFL draft. "This is the best decision for my family and me," Patrick said at the time.

While the NFL projected Patrick as a second-round pick, he believed that once he had the chance to prove himself in front of scouts, he'd move up to the first round.

Clearly Patrick's instincts were just as strong in life as in sports. As he'd predicted, NFL scouts were impressed with Patrick's arm strength. Of course, how couldn't they be? They also loved his mobility and the way he played to win. His stats were obviously incredible. The question was how much of his success in college was because of his talents, and how much of it was because Coach Kingsbury ran such a wide-open offense?

When Coach Kingsbury was an assistant at Texas A&M University, he coached a quarterback named Johnny Manziel, who won the Heisman as the best player in college football. Then in his first season at Texas Tech, Coach Kingsbury had success with Baker Mayfield before he transferred to Oklahoma.

And now Patrick came along and succeeded. Was it the players, or was it the coach?

Patrick thought he was much more than a so-called system quarterback. Yes, Coach Kingsbury drew up great plays that got receivers open, but he also taught Patrick how to play quarterback, not just how to run specific plays.

"Coach Kingsbury took me from an athlete, a baseball player on the field, to making me a quarterback," Patrick said. "He taught me how to go through progressions, taught me to read coverages and just built me up and helped me become a young man."

Now Patrick was determined to prove it. He went to the NFL Combine in February, an annual event where draft prospects are weighed, measured, and put through a series of drills—everything from strength and agility to throwing passes. Patrick, who always thrived on competition, loved it.

He was impressive enough at the Combine that twenty-eight teams came to his "Pro Day" at Texas Tech. A Pro Day is when a school invites scouts to come and watch all of their draft eligible players. It is common for twenty-eight or more teams to go to the Pro Day of college powerhouse teams such as Alabama, Clemson, or LSU. But for a less celebrated program like Tech, which was coming off a 5–7 season, this was a huge turnout. The highlight was when Patrick chucked a pass eighty yards, a feat so impressive that some of the scouts in attendance actually applauded.

After the Combine, Patrick wasn't done yet with the scouting process. He began doing private workouts for individual teams, usually flying to their facility and working out for them and holding a series of meetings with the coach, the general manager, even the owner. Patrick crisscrossed the country all throughout the spring, making eighteen visits, more than any other quarterback in the 2017 NFL draft. He didn't mind.

"It was actually a lot of fun," Patrick said years later. "I got to meet a lot of great coaches and talk a lot of football."

In truth, he didn't need to do all of those things that spring to catch the eye of his future team.

Brett Veach worked in the front office for the Kansas City Chiefs, and his job was to watch lots and lots of college football in search of star players he could bring to the team. During Patrick's sophomore season at Tech, Veach was watching game footage of the Red Raiders. But not really to scout Patrick. He was truly interested in an offensive lineman named Le'Raven Clark. A scout's job is to zero in on a specific player and try to figure out his every strength and weakness. It requires a ton of focus and concentration. It isn't easy.

Yet no matter how much he tried to watch Le'Raven's blocking technique or his footwork, he kept getting distracted by Tech's quarterback. Who, Brett kept thinking, was this kid making amazing throw after amazing throw? Patrick was just a sophomore, so he wasn't eligible to be drafted and thus wasn't really on Brett Veach's radar. Besides, the Chiefs already had a very good quarterback, Alex Smith.

Yet Brett couldn't stop watching the Mahomes Show. He became obsessed with Patrick. Soon he was watching every snap Patrick took at Tech, even scouting footage of him as a freshman. Then he talked with the Chiefs scout for the state of Texas. Then he talked to coaches, friends, even Patrick's parents. He tried to find everything out he could about Patrick.

Although Tech struggled to win games during Patrick's junior season, Brett never stopped watching every snap. He loved everything Patrick did on the field. He was convinced this wasn't a "system" quarterback that Coach Kingsbury had pumped up. He thought this was a special player.

"I thought he could be a [ten- to fifteen-year] starter in the NFL," Veach said. In other words, a guy the Chiefs needed to draft in the first round.

Brett even scouted Patrick in person, including a game at Iowa State in November of his junior season. During the first half, though, Patrick got hit and injured his shoulder. Suddenly Brett thought he'd come all the way to Ames, Iowa, for nothing. Soon Iowa State was leading 45–3. With Tech's season already going bad and Patrick destined to enter the NFL draft, Brett thought Patrick would sit out the rest of the game.

Instead Patrick came back in to play even though there was almost no chance of victory—Iowa State would win 66–10. That didn't matter to Patrick. He couldn't stand to be on the sideline. He just wanted to compete. Brett loved it.

But just because Brett loved Patrick's potential, it didn't mean the Chiefs would be able to land him in the draft.

The NFL sets its draft order by allowing the team with the worst record to pick first, the second worst to pick second, the third worst to pick third, and so on. The Chiefs were a good team. They finished the 2016 season with a 12–4 record, which landed them at the twenty-seventh pick. There was little chance Patrick would still be available at that number.

Kansas City began to plot a way to move up in the draft and get Patrick. To do so, they'd need to trade draft picks with Buffalo, who was selecting tenth. However, they didn't want anyone to know their plan, or even that they were interested in Patrick. If they did, someone might swoop in and steal him.

They had just one meeting with Patrick. Coach Andy Reid spent a lot of time running through potential plays with Patrick. It was a way for Coach Reid to test Patrick's football knowledge. Coach Reid came away impressed. And Patrick began to believe that Kansas City wanted him, even if they didn't say so.

Even though Kansas City already had a starter in Alex Smith, it would make sense for them to draft a quarterback because Alex was not only getting closer to the age when QBs typically retire, but also because he'd proven himself injury prone in the past. KC could develop a young quarterback under Alex's tutelage as Alex continued to be their starter.

Patrick began to dream of playing for the Chiefs and living in a city that was neither too big nor too far from Texas.

"I hoped Kansas City was going to draft me," Patrick said. "I looked at the team and saw the guys they had, the play makers they had. And then the biggest reason was having Coach Reid. I spent five or six hours with him listening to him talk about football. I felt like if I went there he would get the best out of me.

"I had a good hunch they were going to come up and get me."

Patrick's hunch proved correct when Kansas City made the deal on draft night. The Chiefs traded three draft picks, including two first-rounders, to get Patrick. Around the NFL, there were plenty of people questioning what the Chiefs were doing. Why give up so many good draft picks to take a quarterback when they already had a starter? Most teams saw Patrick as a raw talent, not someone who could start right away.

That even included the Chiefs. They planned on having Alex Smith play in the 2017 season while Patrick practiced and learned about the NFL. Drafting Patrick was about the long-term future.

"Right now, Patrick is not ready to play," Coach Reid said after the draft. "He's got some work to do. We have to be patient with him. He's definitely not a finished product right now. But he has tremendous upside."

Although Patrick wanted to play right away, he was willing to sit and learn. He was twenty-one years old when he was drafted and he leaned on the advice of his father and godfather, LaTroy Hawkins, who told him that it wasn't about making a professional sports team, it was about staying on the team.

"Just going out there every single day and trying to maximize every single practice," Patrick said. "That's how I was raised."

After being drafted, one of his more important tasks was picking a jersey number. All Patrick's life he'd worn the number 5. Patrick's father had usually worn number 20 or 23. While he was Patrick's idol, "I didn't want to have the same number as my dad." In fact, he didn't want to have anyone's number.

"I always wanted to do something different," Patrick said. "I didn't want to have the same number as anyone else in the league. I thought number 5 translated to baseball and basketball and football. So I chose that."

The problem? Kansas City's kicker, Cairo Santos, wore number 5. Suddenly Patrick needed a new number.

"My mom said to me, 'You were always number 5, but you were picked number 10. Add them together. How about number 15?'"

And with that, 15 became Patrick's number. Little did anyone know at the time that his number 15 Chiefs jersey would become the best-selling jersey in all the NFL, that kids and adults alike would wear that number all over the world.

At the time, Patrick just wanted to prove that Kansas City made the right decision in drafting him. Even though he wasn't going to play much, throughout his rookie year, he tried to get a little bit better each day. He listened to his coaches. He put in extra work. "He's constantly studying," Coach Reid noted.

He got settled and learned to live on his own. He also learned to live like a pro. In college, he was surrounded by friends, played Wiffle Ball games on campus, and enjoyed being a college kid. In Kansas City it was different. This was a job. He ate healthier. He tried to get more sleep. He even swore off video games, including his favorite, *Call of Duty*, during the season. It was better to study than be distracted. Along the way, he tried to pick up every bit of knowledge he could from Alex Smith, the team's veteran starter.

Alex was thirty-three years old and a former number one overall draft pick. He knew that Patrick was drafted to be his replacement. Yet throughout the season he not only worked to get the Chiefs prepared for that week's game, he was selfless enough to try to help Patrick. If Patrick chose to stay late and watch extra film, Alex would often stay also, offering up pointers.

"I learned a ton from Alex," Patrick said. "The way he was able to go about it as a professional and having a great year. Just seeing how he went about every single day, the game plan, recognizing coverages. He didn't hold anything back from me. He taught me. That's just the type of person he is."

The Chiefs went 10–6 that year. They clinched a spot in the playoffs prior to the regular season finale in Denver. Since it didn't really matter if Kansas City won the game or not, Coach Reid decided to rest most of the starters and give the backups a chance to play. That meant Patrick, who hadn't taken a snap all season, got to start.

It was a cold day in Denver, but Patrick was

excited for his first chance to shine. He made some understandable mistakes, including a bad interception. He also took a couple of sacks.

Yet he mostly showed plenty of promise, going 22 for 35 for 284 yards. And when Denver tied the game up late, Patrick led a game-winning field goal drive, including making an impressive throw across his body while scrambling from the pass rush. Fans were stunned by the play, unaware that such passes would soon become routine from him.

The Chiefs would lose in the first round of the playoffs. Patrick never got on the field. He'd done enough as a rookie, though, to impress Coach Reid and the others. His work ethic. His learning. And that one performance against Denver.

"I came out of that going, 'you know what?'" Coach Reid said. "'This kid is ready to go. He's ready to go ahead and lead.'"

11

Superstar

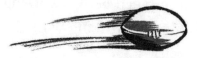

O<small>N</small> J<small>ANUARY</small> 30, 2018, the Kansas City Chiefs traded Alex Smith to Washington in exchange for a cornerback and a draft pick. That meant Patrick Mahomes was now the Chiefs' starting quarterback. Just like when he took over at Whitehouse and at Texas Tech, patience and work had allowed Patrick to prove himself. The chance to lead an NFL team was all his.

No one quite knew what Patrick was capable of, but Coach Reid certainly believed in him enough to trade away a veteran starter.

"He gives you the confidence that he's going to be OK," Coach Reid said.

For Patrick, the run-up to the 2018 season opener somehow felt both familiar and totally new. He loved having a team again, being the leader, having the guys look to him to deliver. That element brought him back to the ball fields of Whitehouse. And while the offense was much more advanced and the competition much better, working with Coach Reid felt a little like working with Coach Cook or Coach Kingsbury.

It was different, too, though. There was more media than he'd ever seen. More attention. More expectations. More everything. The Chiefs don't just have fans in Kansas City, where the only other professional sports team is the MLB Royals. They have supporters all over the region, in Missouri, Kansas, Iowa, even Arkansas and Oklahoma and Nebraska. Then there are all the people who grew up in KC, but moved away.

The fans call themselves "Chiefs Kingdom" and that made sense to Patrick. Every time he turned around, there was another red flag flying symbolizing how important the team was to its fans. He knew they were relying on him.

Before the opening week game at the Los Angeles Chargers, Patrick felt nervous. This wasn't unusual. He was good at shaking off pressure, but he felt it. On game days, he often struggled to eat because of nerves. He would force down a few bites of food because he knew he needed the energy.

"I usually get eggs in the morning, maybe an omelette at most," Patrick said. "If the game is later in the day, I'll try a little bit of spaghetti and maybe a steak."

After the game, he'd usually be starving and eat a huge meal. In Kansas City, he began to find some great barbecue spots to go with family, his girlfriend, or any friends that were in town. They were always more than happy to serve the Chiefs' starting quarterback.

As he dressed for the Chargers game, he found himself leaning back on old rituals to try to make it seem like no big deal. He wanted to make sure he felt comfortable, even in the NFL.

"I'm a little superstitious from my baseball days so I wear the sleeve (on his right throwing arm), the headband, and the wristbands (on both wrists)," Patrick said. "That's what I go with."

What really helped him settle down against

the Chargers was watching one of his teammates in action: Tyreek Hill, a young wide receiver who was believed to be the fastest player in the league. Throughout training camp the two had often connected, with Patrick throwing passes as far as he could only to see Tyreek sprint underneath them for the catch.

In this game, the Chargers got the ball first but were forced to punt. They booted one deep, where Tyreek caught it at the Chiefs' own nine-yard line and promptly ran the other way, too fast for anyone to catch him. He went ninety-one yards for a touchdown and before Patrick even had a chance to step onto the field, Kansas City led 7–zip.

On the first offensive drive, Patrick completed a couple of short passes before he hit Tyreek on a short slant pattern. For a normal receiver, that would have been a five-yard gain. Yet Tyreek turned up field and outran everyone. It was a fifty-eight-yard touchdown pass. Just like that, it was 14–3 and Patrick could exhale.

"I needed to settle down," he said.

Patrick wasn't perfect in the game, but he showed glimmers of the greatness he'd displayed at Tech. He completed just fifteen passes, but four of them were for touchdowns, including two to Tyreek. The

Chiefs won 38–28. Patrick's performance would have been considered great for any quarterback; for a guy making just his second career start, it was incredible.

Up next was a trip to Pittsburgh, where the Chiefs hadn't won in thirty-two years.

The Steelers were led by veteran quarterback and former Super Bowl champ Ben Roethlisberger. Matched up against Patrick, it was a standoff between the longtime talent and the young upstart. Or something like David versus Goliath.

That didn't matter to Patrick, who felt more relaxed and confident. He topped his impressive previous performance, throwing an amazing six touchdown passes in the game, using five different receivers, and KC won a shootout, 42–37. He now had a total of ten touchdowns and no interceptions, the most TDs by a quarterback in the first two weeks of the season in NFL history.

"You never expect to have 10 touchdowns at this point of the season," Patrick said. "But I knew with this offense and the weapons that we have and the scheme Coach Reid has drawn up that we had a chance to be really, really good. The possibilities are endless."

All across the NFL, people began paying attention. Players, coaches, media, fans, you name it, they were talking about this Mahomes kid. It was clear that Coach Reid, Brett Veach, and the rest of the Chiefs' staff had been right about him. Surrounding him with talent such as Tyreek, tight end Travis Kelce, and running back Kareem Hunt just made him that much more dangerous.

In week three: Patrick threw for three touchdowns in a victory over San Francisco. Then came a win at Denver. Then another back home against Jacksonville. The Chiefs were 5–0 and headed for a Sunday-night game at New England. This was huge.

The Sunday-night game is the only game being played at that time and is broadcast nationally on NBC. Millions and millions of people watch it each week. The Patriots were the premier franchise in the league, having won five Super Bowls at that point behind star quarterback Tom Brady and their defensive-wizard coach, Bill Belichick.

For much of the country, this was their first chance to watch Patrick live, and against the mighty Patriots at that. Meanwhile, Patrick and Kansas City knew that if they were going to reach the Super Bowl this year, a prospect that seemed more and more likely each week, they'd probably have to defeat New England in the playoffs to do it.

Before the game, Bill Belichick, who is considered by many to be the best coach in NFL history, was asked what impressed him about Patrick.

"Pretty much everything," Belichick said. "Gets the ball to all of his receivers. Quick. Quick release. [He] sees things quickly. Can extend plays. Got a great arm. Got a fabulous arm. Throws the ball out of the stadium. [He] makes good decisions. Accurate. Gets the ball out on time . . . The farther a quarterback can throw it, the more you gotta defend. If the ball is on their twenty-yard line you still gotta defend to the goal line against him. He can rip it."

Patrick appreciated the kind words but he couldn't worry about praise from the other coach. He had a game to win—and what a game it was. New England jumped out to a 24–9 lead, but the Chiefs kept coming.

Patrick, after all, had never been one to back down.

With just over three minutes to go, Patrick connected with Tyreek on a seventy-five-yard touchdown to tie the score and leave the usually loud Gillette Stadium silent.

For years Patrick had studied Tom Brady, though, so he almost knew what was coming. Their styles of play were different. Tom was more of a traditional, stay-in-the-pocket passer. He was incredibly accurate and never seemed to rattle. Patrick loved his consistency and the way he prepared for defenses. It was on display at the end, when he quickly marched the Pats down the field for a game-winning field goal with no time left. New England won, 43–40.

Despite the loss, all of America was buzzing about Patrick and the Chiefs. Patrick threw thirteen touchdowns over the next four games, all of them victories. He then heaved six TDs in a wild, 54–51 loss on Monday Night Football to the Los Angeles Rams.

Everything was happening fast. Patrick was being swarmed by reporters after games. They were breaking down his plays on ESPN. He appeared on the cover of *Sports Illustrated*. Everyone wanted to know everything about him, from his days back in Whitehouse, Texas, to his habit of putting ketchup on nearly everything he ate, including steak. In KC, barbecue sauce is king. Ketchup?

"I don't think it's that weird," Patrick said with a laugh.

As Patrick racked up wins and touchdowns, his name began popping up in MVP conversations, even though it was just his first season as a starter. It was an incredible rise. Preseason, no one could have imagined this relatively unknown twenty-three-year-old with one career start would be MVP, but each week Patrick did more and more to prove that he was the obvious choice.

Indeed, he would win the award after the season. But Patrick, ever a team player, had his sights set on a much bigger group goal: the Super Bowl.

By the end of the year, the Chiefs were 12–4 and the top seed in their conference, the AFC. Patrick had thrown for 5,097 yards and fifty touchdowns. He was just the second quarterback to have ever thrown for five thousand yards and fifty touchdowns—the other being Peyton Manning. He'd also rushed for 272 yards and two TDs. He was one of the biggest stars in the league. His agent was fielding calls to do major television campaigns, including joining Green Bay quarterback Aaron Rodgers in a series of State Farm commercials. He would also appear on the cover of the Madden 20 video game.

It was all a dream come true, but also a bit of a challenge. Patrick was determined not to let all the praise and attention go to his head. He just wanted to continue to be himself.

"I never want to change my personality," Patrick said. "I want to be the same person now that I was in middle school."

Now it was time for the playoffs. Kansas City had home field advantage and they were eyeing their first Super Bowl since 1970. In their first game, Kansas City easily dispatched Indianapolis 31–13 to set up an AFC Championship Game against, you guessed it, New England. This would be Patrick's greatest challenge.

Everyone wanted to see if Patrick could continue his near perfect season. To do so, he'd have to solve the defensive strategy of Coach Belichick and then unseat Tom Brady, who was forty-one years old at the time, as the best quarterback in the league.

The game was played on a brutally cold January night, with a wind chill that was in single digits. Patrick may have been a sensation, but the Pats were the NFL's dynasty and they never got nervous. They showed it by taking the opening kickoff and having Tom Brady lead a fifteen-play, eighty-yard touchdown drive. By halftime, it was 14–0 New England. The high-powered Chiefs were scoreless after thirty minutes.

Patrick walked through the locker room at halftime and kept reminding his teammates to stick to the plan and keep grinding. The message sunk in. KC cut the lead to 14–7, then 17–14, then took the lead 21–17.

New England wasn't giving up, though, and re-gained the lead, 24–21. Then KC came back, 28–24, but New England was not to be outdone, scoring with 0:39 remaining to take a 31–28 lead.

The game looked over. Patrick had other ideas.

Thirty-nine seconds isn't much, but it was enough for Patrick. He and the Chiefs took possession of the ball on their own thirty-one-yard line with time for just a couple of plays. Patrick threw a deep pass for twenty-one yards. Then another deep one for twenty-seven. Against all odds, with the clock ticking down, the Chiefs were somehow in scoring position.

With just eleven seconds remaining, KC kicked a game-tying field goal. It was an incredible rally.

But would it be the turnaround moment Patrick and KC needed to win the game?

In overtime, the winner of the coin flip gets the ball first, and if they score a touchdown the game is over. New England won that flip and Tom Brady made sure Patrick Mahomes never saw the field again. He led a masterful sixty-five-yard drive on thirteen plays, finishing with a Rex Burkhead touchdown to win the game.

It was a bitter defeat for the Chiefs, 37–31. The Super Bowl was so close, yet so far away. Chiefs fans and players were frustrated that Patrick and the offense never got a chance in overtime. To make matters worse, they had to watch New England go on and win their sixth Super Bowl a couple of weeks later.

It was a lesson for Patrick, though. Don't leave anything up to chance. After the game against the Patriots, he sat in the Chiefs locker room at Arrowhead Stadium, dejected and depressed. That's when a security guard came up and said he had an unlikely visitor.

Right then Tom Brady, still wearing his Patriots uniform, appeared. Players don't often go into the other team's locker room, especially after what would be a heart-wrenching loss for the Chiefs. But Tom was an NFL legend, respected by all. He was on his way to another Super Bowl title, but he recognized the incredible talent of his young competitor that day. It was almost like Tom knew that at his age, his time atop the mountain would be ending soon and Patrick's starting just as quickly.

"He's a great player," Tom said.

It was the highest praise possible for Patrick, who said Tom sat with him for a bit and offered some advice for the rest of his career.

"The biggest thing he said was, 'stay with the process and be who you are,'" Patrick told *NBC Sports*. "He didn't want me to change at all. He wanted me to go out there and take advantage of every single day. When you hear it from a guy like that, who's had the success at the level he's had for his entire career, you know you've got to take advantage of every single day if you want to be great."

12

Champion

PATRICK MAHOMES lined up behind his center to receive the snap. It was 4th and 1 from the Denver five-yard line. This was Week 7 of the 2019 season, Patrick's second as the starting quarterback, and the Chiefs led 10–6 in the second quarter. Patrick knew what to do. Keep the drive going, punch in a touchdown, and Kansas City was well on its way to a 5–2 record, eyes still on the Super Bowl.

Patrick took the snap and immediately pushed forward into his offensive line, which was grunting and shoving the Denver defense back. By the time

Patrick's momentum was stopped, he'd gained two yards on the QB sneak. First down, Chiefs.

Yet as players began to roll off the pile, it was clear the yards had come with a price. Patrick was down, in pain, grabbing his right knee. He took off his helmet and clutched his face. Teammates looked on in fear. The Kansas City training staff charged out to assess the damage.

All over Chiefs Kingdom, heck, all over the entire NFL, everyone was holding their breath. No one wanted to see this . . . Patrick Mahomes injured. He had already been dealing with pain in his ankle, but this appeared much worse.

Eventually Patrick would hobble off the field and into the locker room. He was soon diagnosed with a dislocated kneecap, a painful injury, but one that he could recover from fairly quickly. It could have been much worse. He would be back, doctors said. This year even, as long as physical therapy went well.

"I had no idea what was going to happen," Patrick said. "But our training staff pushed me to be great every single day."

It was a strange time for Patrick. His life and football career had been moving one hundred miles per hour. Big wins. Big awards. Big fanfare. If he wasn't playing on national television, he was in a commercial on national television. He'd become an overnight celebrity, his signature haircut and memorable smile making him hard to miss.

And then, all of sudden, for the first time in his athletic career, he was injured to the point that he couldn't play. Desperate to get back as soon as possible, he dove in with the training staff. If anything, his time off the field reminded him how special it is to have the opportunity to play competitive sports.

"I just wanted to get back out there and be with the guys," Patrick said.

Three weeks later, after an intense rehab process, he was. Patrick and the Chiefs lost that day, to Tennessee, but he went 36 for 50 for 446 yards and three touchdowns. Those were on par with pre-injury Patrick Mahomes stats, and a signal that he'd made a strong recovery. The knee looked good. It felt good. Now Patrick was as determined as ever to win Kansas City its first Super Bowl in fifty years.

Patrick was every bit as good in 2019 as he was in 2018. His numbers were down, in part because of the injury, but his command on the field was every bit as impressive. He threw for 4,031 yards and twenty-six touchdowns. He wasn't named league MVP—that went to Baltimore quarterback Lamar Jackson—but Patrick had always been much more focused on victories and team accomplishments.

The truth was, he thought he'd become a better player, more in line with the kind of quarterback Tom Brady was. He now had some experience and had improved at reading defenses and anticipating blitzes and coverages. He thought he was ready to win a Super Bowl, which was all that matters.

"I know for sure mentally I'm better," Patrick said. "I'm recognizing defensive protections faster. It's hard to put those numbers up [like 2018], but as a team we found a way to win."

The Chiefs went 12–4 and entered the playoffs as one of the favorites to win it all. They had even gone to New England during Week 14 and defeated the Patriots, 23–16, a victory that felt important if only to prove that KC could stand up to the champions.

"It was a big step just getting over that hump," Patrick said. "I think for me to kind of have that win over that team was big. It started the momentum for us."

In the playoff opener, though, KC's hopes seemed to be quickly dashed as they trailed Houston

24–0 in the second quarter. Fans watching at home and in person began to panic.

But not Patrick Mahomes. He kept his teammates relaxed, reminding them on the sideline that there was plenty of time to come back.

They took it one possession at a time. Patrick never faltered or doubted his squad's ability to be the first NFL team in eight years to overcome a twenty-one-point first-quarter deficit. That calm demeanor paid off.

KC's offense was electric, scoring touchdowns on seven straight drives, including four in the second quarter to lead 28–24 at halftime. KC further reversed course from there, turning what had started out as a nightmare into a commanding victory, 51–31. Patrick accounted for 321 yards passing and five touchdowns.

The following week, in the AFC Championship Game, the Chiefs hosted the Tennessee Titans, which had entered the playoffs as underdogs and gone on to upset two Super Bowl favorites, the New England Patriots and the Baltimore Ravens.

There would be no Tom Brady to go through this season for the Chiefs. Instead Tennessee came to Arrowhead Stadium and led 10–0 and then 17–7.

It was like the Houston game all over again. Would Tennessee knock yet another powerhouse out of the playoffs? Or could KC come back . . . again?

The answer? Of course. This was Patrick Mahomes at his finest.

Patrick hit Tyreek for a twenty-yard touchdown, rushed for a twenty-seven-yard TD on his own and then threw a sixty-yarder to Sammy Watkins as the Chiefs rolled to a 35–24 victory. No need for overtime. No need for terrifying final moments like in last year's AFC Championship. This time KC was headed to the Super Bowl.

The NFL quickly built a stage on the field and Patrick went up there to accept the Lamar Hunt Trophy on behalf of his team for being the champions of the AFC. Lamar Hunt, for whom the award was named, had owned the Chiefs for decades. His son Clark was now in charge. The Kansas City fans, who had waited half a century for a Super Bowl trip, roared as Patrick held the trophy above his head.

"I had no words up there on that stage," Patrick said. "Having that Lamar Hunt trophy come back to Kansas City and to see every person in that stadium stay . . . it was incredible."

Reaching the Super Bowl was an accomplishment

in itself. Patrick, like most Americans, had grown up watching the game, attending parties, and laughing at the best commercials.

Now he was the star of the show. He would go through the annual circus of media day, with cameras on him around the clock. He would run out onto the field, the Super Bowl emblem at its very center. He would know that all eyes were on him.

It was exciting. His family flew in for the game. So did his girlfriend and some high school buddies. Coach Kingsbury, who was now the head coach of the NFL's Arizona Cardinals, bought a ticket to watch his old player. Also in attendance: Coach Adam Cook, plus high school teammates Ryan Cheatham, Jake Parker, and Coleman Patterson. No one wanted to miss seeing Patrick in the Super Bowl.

The game was held in Miami. While that meant warm weather, beaches, and lots of fun for most people, it was all work, no play for Patrick and the Chiefs. They didn't just want to reach the Super Bowl, they wanted to win it. That meant focusing on the task at hand, namely defeating the San Francisco 49ers and their stingy defense.

Heading into the game, the media focused on the 49ers' defensive line, dubbing it the best Patrick had ever faced. If he could deal with their relentless pressure, they said, then the Chiefs had a chance. If not, the 49ers would probably win. This was the key to the game.

The matchup was neck and neck from the start, with the Chiefs initially gaining the upper hand early, only to quickly give way to a 49ers lead that expanded to 20–10 by the fourth quarter. With 8:53 remaining in the game, San Francisco's pass rush had gotten the best of Patrick and the Chiefs, and it looked like the media's prediction would come true. Patrick had been sacked three times and intercepted twice. His Kansas City offense hadn't scored a point since kicking a field goal late in the first quarter. Nearly thirty minutes of game time, and a couple of hours of real time, had passed since then.

Patrick was en route to his worst performance in his biggest game as a professional. The Super Bowl clock was dwindling by the second.

"I was making a lot of mistakes," Mahomes said.

The Chiefs were getting the ball back, though, on their own seventeen-yard line. It was perhaps their last chance to get the offense going and still win the Super Bowl. It wouldn't be easy. This was the fifty-fourth Super Bowl ever held, and only twice had a team rallied from ten or more points down in the fourth quarter to win. Both times it had been Tom Brady's Patriots.

Facing that daunting reality and the pressure of the moment, Patrick remained upbeat. While this demeanor would surprise fans that didn't know him, for anyone who did, it was expected. He gathered his teammates together with a simple message.

"They are going to talk about this [game]," he told them, "for a long time."

This was exactly what his offense wanted to hear and needed to hear from their leader. Soon Patrick was scrambling for a first down. Then he hit Tyreek for another. Then facing 3rd and 15, he dropped way behind the line of scrimmage to buy time from the pass rush and flicked a pass sixty yards in the air to an open Tyreek. It went for a forty-four-yard gain.

A couple of plays later, Patrick threw a touchdown pass to finish off a ten-play, eighty-three-yard drive. Suddenly the San Francisco lead was down to 20–17. There was still 6:13 remaining in the game.

After the 49ers were forced to quickly punt, Patrick geared up the offense again, this time from the Chiefs' thirty-five-yard line. He was feeling it now, in a groove and sure of himself. It was like he was flinging it around Whitehouse High School again. He hit Tyreek. Then Travis. Then Tyreek again. Then Sammy Watkins got open for a thirty-eight-yard gain. A couple of plays later, another TD pass, and KC had the lead.

It took just 6:16 for the Chiefs to go from nearly hopeless to in the lead. Patrick Mahomes, number 15, had upended the entire Super Bowl.

"They can score very fast," said San Francisco's coach, Kyle Shanahan.

The Chiefs would score again for good measure, pouring on the final twenty-one points of the game to win the Super Bowl, 31–20. It was their third playoff game, and their third come-from-behind playoff win. Patrick was named the game's MVP after throwing for two touchdowns and rushing for another.

"I have the mindset that I'm going to just keep firing it," he said.

Confetti fell all around him. He sought out his family and friends, teammates and coaches, to celebrate. He sought out all the people who'd long seen promise in him—not just his parents, but Little League teammates and youth coaches, all the way up to Coach Reid. It wasn't just the athletic talent, it was the humility, the work ethic, the person he'd always been and would become.

He was just twenty-four years old, but it had felt like a long time coming.

"He's just an amazing young man," Coach Adam Cook said. "Every good thing that happens for him, he's earned. He really has."

Back in high school, Patrick had watched the Super Bowl and noticed that the Super Bowl MVP every year gets to appear in a commercial for Disney World. The spot gets taped right after the game, right on the field. They get paid money to do it, but the best part might be the free trip to Disney World in Orlando, Florida.

In high school, Patrick had tweeted: "I bet it feels amazing to be the quarterback who says, 'I'm going to Disney World' after winning the Super Bowl."

Now, after Patrick had actually won the Super Bowl and was named MVP, he was approached on the field by a camera crew from the Walt Disney Company. He jumped at the chance to say the famous line. He even recalled his old tweet.

With his teammates celebrating around him, Patrick looked into the camera and shouted, "I'm going to Disney World!" Two days later, he was there, leading the Disney World parade.

One more dream accomplished for Patrick Mahomes, who won't stop working no matter how many he achieves.

Instant
Replay

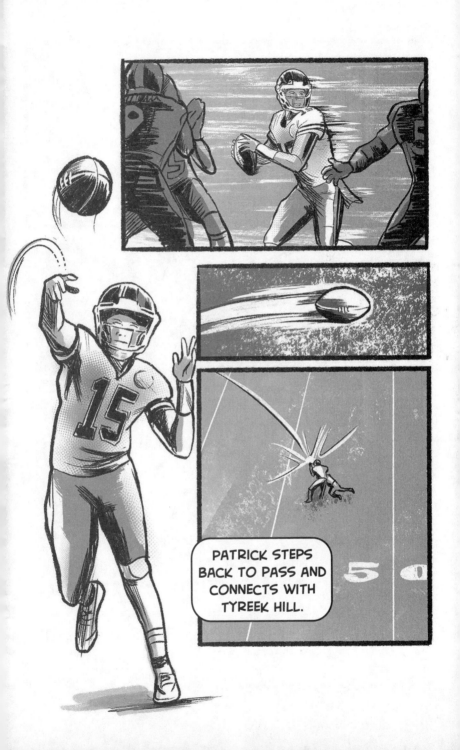

PATRICK STEPS BACK TO PASS AND CONNECTS WITH TYREEK HILL.

AFTER A PENALTY AND LOSS OF YARDS, THE CHIEFS GAIN GROUND ON A PASS TO TRAVIS KELCE.

KAREEM HUNT RUNS THE BALL TO THE ONE-YARD LINE.

A PERFECT STRIKE TO DEMETRIUS HARRIS PUTS THE CHIEFS IN THE RED ZONE.

Hungry for More EPIC ATHLETES?
Look Out for These Superstar
Biographies, in Stores Now!